"What I have always adored about Stephanie is that somehow her energy and positive spirit are just as compelling as her over-the-top delicious food. With *Gather & Graze*, she shares all of that brilliant, fun-loving flavor and cooking intel that have made her such a shining star in the food world and her restaurants so coveted. Her recipes and menus are casual, craveable, and most of all doable. I dare you to open this book and not want to cook everything!"

—GAIL SIMMONS, FOOD EXPERT, TV HOST, AND AUTHOR OF *BRINGING IT HOME: FAVORITE RECIPES FROM A LIFE OF ADVENTUROUS EATING*

"I've been a huge fan of Stephanie's from the very first bite I took at Girl & the Goat, and my love for her as a chef and a person has steadily grown ever since. Getting married and starting a family may have been the best thing that ever happened to her as a successful entrepreneur, focusing her intensity and realizing that time poverty was part of the new equation. One of the best books on cooking at home is one of the results of that math. *Gather & Graze* not only is filled with spectacular recipes that will delight the home cook, but the way the food fits into all our lives, coming together to share, is the real genius of this superbly crafted book. This isn't a show-offy book either, it's a real-life primer on the best way to eat and entertain for family, friends, and loved ones."

—ANDREW ZIMMERN

"Stephanie Izard is one of the most uniquely talented and vivacious chefs working today, and she's managed to capture so much of what makes her food special on these pages."

—ALTON BROWN

Gather & Graze

GATHER & GRAZE

120 FAVORITE RECIPES FOR TASTY GOOD TIMES

Stephanie Izard
OF **GIRL & THE GOAT**
WITH **RACHEL HOLTZMAN**

PHOTOGRAPHS BY **HUGE GALDONES**
FOOD STYLING BY **JOHANNA LOWE**

CLARKSON POTTER/PUBLISHERS
NEW YORK

THIS BOOK IS DEDICATED TO
MY MOM, SUE. TO THIS DAY,
I STILL ASK MY DAD TO GO
THROUGH HER BOOKS AND
FILES AND SEND ME HER
RECIPES. I KNOW SHE WOULD
HAVE PROUDLY ADDED
THIS COOKBOOK TO HER
COLLECTION.

CONTENTS

INTRODUCTION

THE PAST SIX YEARS HAVE BEEN A WHIRLWIND: I OPENED MY CHICAGO restaurant Girl & the Goat, added a diner across the street called Little Goat, ate my weight in dumplings in China, and opened a third restaurant inspired by my love of all things Chinese-ish, Duck Duck Goat. But two of the most awesome things to happen were meeting the love of my life, Gary Valentine, and having our son, Ernie.

Five years ago, Gary and I were introduced by mutual friends and we instantly hit it off. He was the beer expert around town, and what goes better with a chef than a brewer? It was a match made in food-nerd heaven. His people were my people: beer folks like to eat and chefs love to drink. A year later, we got married—Strawberry Nesquik and Cheez-It wedding cake and all—and we've been feeding people and plying them with liquor together ever since. In May of 2016, we welcomed Ernie into the mix.

Let's just say that B.E. (Before Ernie), entertaining looked a little different. These days we start (and end) a little earlier, but we've definitely upped our game—especially because it means having people come to us, instead of going out. Whether it's brunch on a Sunday Funday or hosting an openhouse Fourth of July party, we like bringing our "work" home. And we've learned that keeping things simple and casual is not only easier for us but also more enjoyable for our guests. I see what looks good at the market, then pick out a few of my favorite dishes that people can casually eat—usually standing up—whether it's a fun spin on diner food, like Crumpets with Chorizo Maple Syrup (page 22); a recipe inspired by a recent trip, like "This Little Piggy Went to China" (Szechuan-Style Breakfast Biscuits, page 13); or something straight off the Girl & the Goat menu, like Roasted Shishito Peppers with Sesame Miso and Parmesan (page 195). One of us will be chopping while the other one is stir-frying or grilling. He'll throw me a bowl; I'll toss him the tongs. We're totally that couple—I lose stuff; he finds it. I walk the dog; he picks up the poop. I put Ernie to bed; he cleans up more poop. Team Valentine! And by the time people come over, there's something for them to snack on, sip on, or get involved with, like assembling the ultimate ice cream sundae (complete with homemade ice cream and toppings; page 247) or making from-scratch Masa Chips (page 167), a total crowd-pleaser.

But this book is not an excuse for a bunch of theme-y menus with expected, cheesy food (unless you mean actual cheese, in which case, I lied). On the contrary, this book is a way for me to share all the dishes that have become cult favorites at my restaurants, and break them down so that you can re-create them in your own kitchen. After all, these dishes are just as much at home at a casual picnic/holiday party/Tuesday night dinner for two as they are on a restaurant menu. I've always believed in making comfortable, approachable food, regardless of whether I'm at work or cooking for friends.

People are always asking me what kind of food I cook. To that I say, "delicious food." Yes, I use a lot of Asian ingredients, but that doesn't mean I cook only "Asian" food, whatever that means. Instead, I like to think of each of my ingredients as straight-up flavors. Need something salty? Miso. Funky? Fish sauce. Sweet? Hoisin. Tart? Tamarind. Blend that miso with blue cheese and you have the most insanely tasty dressing of all time. Throw that same miso into a dessert, and it's like eating a rich butterscotch. Introduce tamarind to some sexy, fatty bacon, and suddenly the world's a much better place.

What I cook is what I just plain like. I take inspiration from everything around me—my travels, my chefs, Gary, my dog Burt, you name it—and give it my own spin. So maybe it's not the most traditional (my okra on the grill has southerners clutching their pearls; no one in China uses fish sauce on their dumplings; and I've never been to Italy, but I really like my made-up salsa verde—see Sauce Green, page 133). But at the end of the day, it's all about hitting that sweet, salty, savory, tangy, saucy spot that answers all your hungry prayers.

In this book, I not only share these recipes—which people have been asking me for since I first opened Girl & the Goat—but I also give you the tools and tips to make them your own. I walk you through basic techniques and highlight the simple things you can do that go a long way (hello, marinade), and introduce you to all the goodness that happens when you get past your fears and make things from scratch. Seriously, I don't know where I'd be in life without homemade spice blends like *ras al hanout* (or "Razzle," as we like to call it; see page 43). And

a quick pickle? It's literally just boiling water, sugar, and salt, poured over vegetables. Plus there are helpful nuggets about cooking techniques for things like grilling and making eggs (once the bane of my existence) and how to put recipe components to use for more than one dish (unused marinade + mayo = instant dressing or sauce).

Throughout the book, I sprinkle in notes on some of my favorite pantry staples, like fish sauce, malt vinegar, miso, fermented tofu, sorrel, and hoisin sauce. A little bit of funky, salty, sweet, or vinegary goodness goes a very long way in a dish; I give tips for using these unique flavors in things like sauces, marinades, and dressings.

I also give lots of options for making these recipes as simple as possible, especially if it's a busy weeknight. You'll notice I always call for eating family style because I've always been a big fan of putting out a bunch of food that everyone can share versus dainty little plates with, like, a quail leg and the world's tiniest tuft of herbs. That's not how I serve food in my restaurants, and it's definitely not how I feed my friends when they come over. Keep it simple, spread it all on a platter, and let everyone load up on one plate. It's more fun for them, and fewer dishes for you! The menus at the end of each chapter are suggestions; they can be stripped down for parts or substituted—for instance, I point out what components of a recipe you can just go buy at the store instead. In short, these recipes can be as difficult or as easy as you want to make them. Is buying a tub of ricotta instead of making it all that stands between you and a nervous breakdown? Save yourself and buy it!

Ultimately, this book is about having fun while making something tasty to eat. At Girl & the Goat (or Big Goat, as we started calling it now that it has a little brother), the most important question our servers ask our guests isn't "How is the food?" It's "Are you having a good time?" I've literally made it my business to make sure people are relaxed and enjoying themselves, and this book is my way of helping you take a little piece of that enjoyment home with you.

BRUNCHING

SZECHUAN-STYLE
BREAKFAST BISCUITS............ *13*

TASTY EGGY KIMCHI
BACON THING *14*

STEAK AND EGGS
with Moroccan Chermoula............ *17*

CORNCAKES AND EGGS
with Heirlooms and Herbs *18*

OOEY-GOOEY
CINNAMON ROLLS *20*

CRUMPETS
with Chorizo Maple Syrup *22*

PERFECT PANCAKES,
TWO WAYS.................. *25*

BISCUITS
with Sausage and
Mushroom Gravy *28*

CREPES
with Spring Onion Cream Cheese *31*

POACHED EGGS
with Tomato-Melon-Apricot
Sofrito *34*

Sunday Funday

Pork Belly Frittata *39*

Smoked Salmon Toast with
Chile-Lime Vinaigrette *40*

Razzle Home Fries *42*

Scones of All Sorts *44*

These Are My Jams *47*

Sweet Cream *49*

Bloody Marys with Blue
Cheese–Stuffed Olives *50*

I COULDN'T DO A BOOK WITHOUT A CHAPTER ON BRUNCH—I OWN A diner! And since I opened Little Goat, brunch has become a very big part of my world. I knew we'd need to offer classic brunch dishes, but I wanted to put our spin on them and challenge people to pick something they might not usually order. So, you'll find steak and eggs, but they're topped with a fresh, herby Moroccan chermoula. There are pancakes, but instead of the usual Bisquick–fake syrup combo, they're made with a sourdough starter, slathered with buttermilk butter, and topped with oatmeal crumble.

But brunch is meant to be comfort food, so we don't get *too* crazy. A lot of times when there's a chef-driven brunch menu, it's got all kinds of fussy, composed plates, and that's not really what it's about. Whether it's to spend time with friends and family or nurse a hangover, brunch should be a special, relaxing weekend thing that you look forward to.

Cheddar-Scallion Biscuits, homemade (page 30) or store-bought

2 tablespoons hoisin sauce, homemade (page 67) or store-bought

1 cup mayonnaise

1 cup Szechuan Chile Sauce (page 127)

¼ cup maple syrup

4 (3-ounce) Chinese sausage patties

Canola oil, if needed

4 large eggs

½ pint blackberries, halved

This is a riff on the classic sausage biscuit, China style. Or as I call it in the restaurant, "This Little Piggy Went to China." I slather a cheddar-scallion biscuit with hoisin mayo (because it makes *everything* better), top it with a nice, big Szechuan sausage patty, add a fried egg, and drown the whole thing in Szechuan Chile Sauce that's been sweetened with a little maple syrup (you know, for breakfast). Then I finish it off with some blackberries to bring that bright acidity. Don't be shy about picking this guy up to eat it, but a knife and fork can be useful. *Makes 4 sandwiches*

SZECHUAN-STYLE BREAKFAST BISCUITS

Preheat the oven to 325°F.

Lightly warm the biscuits in the oven.

In a small bowl, mix the hoisin sauce and mayonnaise. In another small bowl, whisk together the chile sauce and maple syrup.

Heat a large nonstick pan over medium heat and brown the patties until cooked through, 6 to 7 minutes on both sides. If the patties are still a bit soft in the middle, you can transfer the pan to the oven for a few minutes to finish.

Slice each biscuit in half and spread the bottom with the hoisin mayo. Top with a cooked sausage patty.

Reheat the pan over medium-low heat. If there is not enough rendered fat still in the bottom, coat with a little oil. Crack the eggs into the pan and slowly and gently allow the whites to cook all the way through while the yolks remain runny. You don't need to flip the eggs or move them in any way. Use a spatula to carefully transfer the eggs to the top of each sausage patty.

Drizzle the egg-topped patties with the sauce and add a sprinkle of blackberries. Put the other half of the biscuit on top and serve immediately.

This less than traditional brunch item is inspired by a Thai street food dish called *hoi tod*. I once made it for a cooking competition and said that I'd eaten it in Thailand, but I lied. I'd been there, but I had only seen people cooking it at their little stands. But when I got home I immediately watched a video to learn how to make it. A pillowy, crispy-edged crepe (kinda like a cross between funnel cake and a pancake), *hoi tod* is made from a fish sauce–flavored batter. It traditionally has mussels cooked into it, but I didn't know if the Chicago public was ready for that. So I subbed in the chopped-up bacon, added some eggs to make it more breakfasty, included some kimchi for spice, and served it with nuoc cham, a Vietnamese dipping sauce that's usually mostly fish sauce, but I added some malt vinegar to mellow it out. When it came time to name it, I couldn't really think of anything clever or interesting, but I figured I'd eat a dish with all these things in it, so there it was. *Serves 4*

TASTY EGGY KIMCHI BACON THING

Make the batter:
In a large bowl, whisk together the all-purpose flour, rice flour, cornstarch, baking powder, and sugar. In a separate large bowl, whisk together the eggs, fish sauce, and 3 cups cold water. Add to the flour mixture, whisking until incorporated and smooth.

Make the dipping sauce:
In a medium bowl, whisk together all the ingredients.

Make the crepes:
Heat a medium nonstick sauté pan over high heat. Add the oil and then pour 1½ cups of the batter into the pan. Sprinkle in half the kimchi and bacon, then crack 2 eggs directly into the cooking batter. Cook until edges begin to brown, 3 to 4 minutes, before flipping. Cook until center is firm, another 3 to 4 minutes, and then transfer the crepe to a cutting board and cut into pizza-like slices. Repeat.

Toss together the sprouts, cilantro, and sorrel and serve with the crepes and dipping sauce.

BATTER

1 cup all-purpose flour

1 cup rice flour

1 cup cornstarch

¼ cup baking powder

2 teaspoons sugar

4 large eggs

2 tablespoons fish sauce

DIPPING SAUCE

½ cup fresh lemon juice

½ cup fish sauce

5 tablespoons malt vinegar

½ cup dark brown sugar

2 garlic cloves, minced

CREPES

1 tablespoon canola oil

1 cup Kimchi (page 259)

8 slices of bacon, cooked until crisp and cut into 1-inch pieces (about 1 cup)

4 large eggs

2 cups mung bean sprouts

¼ cup roughly chopped fresh cilantro

¼ cup roughly chopped fresh sorrel or basil

1 bunch of cilantro, thick stems removed, leaves roughly chopped

1 bunch of flat-leaf parsley, thick stems removed, leaves roughly chopped

⅓ cup brine-packed small capers

½ tablespoon cumin seeds

1 teaspoon black pepper, plus more for seasoning meat

½ teaspoon cayenne pepper

3 tablespoons grated lemon zest

1½ tablespoons fresh lemon juice

¾ cup extra-virgin olive oil

1 pound skirt steak

Kosher salt

2 tablespoons canola oil

8 large eggs

Sometimes when I feel that I need some fresh inspiration, I'll say "pick a country!" to all the cooks and servers. Then I go on a big kick of learning all about the food there. One time Morocco got shouted out, which is how I came up with our Razzle Spice Mix (page 43) and this chermoula sauce. It's salty and herbaceous, delicious on everything from pork to seafood to eggs, and even great as a marinade for steak. It also makes me think of green eggs and ham. (Okay, green eggs and steak, but close enough!) You could present this dish as a big platter of food with a serving fork or serve it with tortillas and invite your guests to make little breakfast tacos. *Serves 4*

STEAK AND EGGS
with MOROCCAN CHERMOULA

In a blender, combine the cilantro, parsley, capers, cumin seeds, black pepper and cayenne, lemon zest and juice, olive oil, and 2 tablespoons water. Blend until smooth.

Preheat a grill or grill pan to medium-high heat.

Season the steak with salt and pepper. Grill for 3 to 4 minutes on both sides, until medium-rare.

Heat the oil in a large, nonstick sauté pan over medium-high heat. Fry or scramble the eggs, seasoning them with salt and pepper to taste.

Slice the steak against the grain into thin strips. Top with the eggs, and drizzle with the sauce. Serve hot.

I wanted to come up with the perfect cornbread to serve at Girl & the Goat—one that wasn't too dry or wet, too sweet or salty. So, I researched a bunch of recipes, asking all the cooks for their versions, looking at ones we'd done before, and scouring the internet. Then I was watching the Sally Field movie called *Hello, My Name is Doris*, and she made blueberry cornbread. I thought, *Yes, that's it!* I paired blueberries with pickled peppers to round out the sweetness and used a combination of butter and olive oil, each of which adds richness in its own way. I also used a mixture of stone-ground yellow cornmeal for moisture and locally grown blue cornmeal for texture and that pretty blue color. (You could use all yellow cornmeal; just don't use all blue or your cornbread will be dry.) At Little Goat, I bake the batter into corncakes and top them with eggs (cooked any way you like), avocado, crispy bacon, and an heirloom tomato salad—kinda like a BLT gone wild. *Serves 4*

CORNCAKES AND EGGS
WITH HEIRLOOMS AND HERBS

Preheat the oven to 350°F.

Make the corncakes:
In a medium bowl, whisk together the eggs, buttermilk, milk, melted butter, olive oil, and brown sugar.

In a separate large bowl, whisk together the flour, cornmeals, baking powder, and salt. Add the egg mixture and blend well. Use a rubber spatula to fold in the berries and pickled peppers.

Grease a muffin top tin or shallow muffin pan and fill each cup two-thirds full with batter. You should have 8 cakes. Bake until a toothpick inserted in the center comes out clean, 20 minutes. Let the corncakes cool slightly, then remove them from the pan.

Heat the canola oil in a large, nonstick sauté pan over medium-high heat. Fry or scramble the eggs; season with salt and pepper.

Top each warm corncake with some avocado, bacon, and an egg. Garnish with the salad.

CORNCAKES

4 large eggs

1 cup buttermilk

¾ cup whole milk

10 tablespoons unsalted butter, melted

2 tablespoons extra-virgin olive oil

1¾ cups light brown sugar

3¾ cups all-purpose flour

¾ cup yellow cornmeal, fine to medium grind

¾ cup blue cornmeal, fine to medium grind

1 tablespoon baking powder

2½ teaspoons kosher salt

1 cup fresh blueberries

½ cup drained Pickled Hungarian Hots and Bananas (page 262)

2 tablespoons canola oil

8 large eggs

Kosher salt and pepper

Avocado Smash (page 169)

8 slices of bacon, cooked until crisp

Heirlooms and Herb Salad (recipe follows)

Heirlooms and Herb Salad

When little Sun Gold tomatoes are in season, their bright tanginess just pops in your mouth. I love pairing them with juicy heirloom tomatoes and in-season corn, which shows off the different varieties and textures of corn in the Corncakes and Eggs.

Serves 4

1 pint Sun Gold cherry tomatoes, quartered

1 medium heirloom tomato, medium diced

¼ cup fresh basil leaves

2 tablespoons chopped scallions (green part only)

2 tablespoons extra-virgin olive oil

1 tablespoon red wine vinegar

1 tablespoon fish sauce

Kosher salt

In a large bowl, gently toss together the tomatoes, basil, scallions, olive oil, vinegar, and fish sauce. Season to taste with salt and serve immediately.

My mom used to buy those refrigerated cinnamon rolls—the ones where you'd get enough dough to make seven buns and then a teeny-tiny tube of sauce. And I'd use it all on mine. I decided that if I was going to make my own cinnamon buns, then they needed to meet two criteria: they had to be giant, and they had to have an obscene amount of frosting. I prepare ours with brioche dough so they're not too sweet, making them the perfect complement to the two ramekins of sauce poured over the top. *Makes 12 rolls*

OOEY-GOOEY CINNAMON ROLLS

Make the filling:

Whisk together the brown sugar, cinnamon, and cocoa. Add the butter and stir until the mixture is smooth and well combined.

Make the brioche:

In a stand mixer fitted with the paddle attachment, combine the milk, honey, sugar, yeast, and 1 cup of the flour. Mix until well combined and the mixture resembles a very thick batter. Cover the bowl with plastic wrap and let the dough sit at room temperature for 4 to 6 hours, until at least double in size.

Attach a dough hook to the mixer and reattach the bowl with the brioche sponge (mixture). Add the eggs, salt, and remaining 3 cups flour, and mix for 10 minutes. While the mixer is still running, add the butter cubes bit by bit. Once the butter has been incorporated, scrape the dough into a bowl greased with butter, cover loosely with plastic wrap, and refrigerate for 1 hour.

The dough will have grown considerably. Turn it out onto a clean, lightly floured surface. Fold it in half lengthwise and then crosswise, as though you were folding a piece of paper into a square. Put the dough back in the bowl lightly, grease the top of the dough with more butter, and cover the bowl with plastic. Allow the dough to rest in the refrigerator for at least 6 hours and up to 24 hours.

FILLING

3½ cups dark brown sugar

3 tablespoons ground cinnamon

2 teaspoons unsweetened cocoa powder

4 tablespoons (½ stick) unsalted butter, at room temperature

BRIOCHE

½ cup whole milk, at room temperature

1 tablespoon honey

⅔ cup granulated sugar

1½ tablespoons active dry yeast

4 cups all-purpose flour, plus more for shaping

6 large eggs

1½ tablespoons salt

12 tablespoons (1½ sticks) unsalted butter, at room temperature, cut into cubes, plus extra for greasing the bowl and the dough

FROSTING

1 cup (2 sticks) unsalted butter, at room temperature

8 ounces cream cheese, at room temperature

4½ cups confectioners' sugar

1 tablespoon fresh lemon juice

1 tablespoon vanilla extract

Turn out the dough onto a clean, lightly floured surface. Roll it into a 24-inch-long rectangle, about ½ inch thick. Spread a thin, even layer of the butter over the dough and sprinkle with the filling, leaving a ½-inch border around the edges. Gently roll the dough into a 24-inch-long tube. Pinch the lengthwise edges to seal. Slice the tube into 12 (2-inch-thick) rolls. Put the rolls flat side down on a parchment-lined sheet tray, 2 inches apart. Cover lightly with plastic wrap and allow to rest at room temperature for 1 hour.

Make the frosting:
In a stand mixer fitted with the paddle attachment, beat the butter and cream cheese until light in color, about 2 minutes. Reduce the speed to low and add the confectioners' sugar, lemon juice, and vanilla. Mix until well incorporated.

Preheat the oven to 350°F.

Bake the cinnamon rolls until golden brown and fluffy, 10 to 15 minutes. Allow the rolls to cool slightly on the sheet tray, then frost and serve warm.

This is by far our most underrated dish at Little Goat, probably because when people think about crumpets, they imagine dried-out English muffins from the store. But these are made from a yeast-risen pancake batter that gets fried in a pan. They're super-crunchy on the outside and soft and doughy on the inside, ready to soak up tons of chorizo-infused maple syrup. This is a dish that really benefits from the sweet freshness of fruit, so serve it with whatever's in season and looking good. *Serves 6*

CRUMPETS
WITH CHORIZO MAPLE SYRUP

Make the crumpet batter:

In a large bowl, whisk together the milk, olive oil, sugar, yeast, and ½ cup warm water. Cover the bowl with plastic wrap and set the mixture aside for 5 minutes.

In a separate medium bowl, whisk together the flours and salt. Add the flour mixture to the milk mixture and use a wooden spoon to stir until combined.

In a small bowl, combine the baking soda with ½ cup warm water. Add the baking soda mixture to the batter and stir to combine. Cover the bowl with plastic wrap and put in a draft-free spot for 1 hour. The batter should rise slightly and begin to bubble.

Make the chorizo maple syrup:

In a small saucepan over medium heat, heat the canola oil and add the chorizo. Cook, breaking it up with a wooden spoon, until the chorizo is completely cooked through, about 10 minutes. Drain off half the fat and reduce the heat to low. Stir in the mustard and soy sauce, and then add the maple syrup. Allow the syrup to steep over low heat for 10 minutes. Hold over the lowest heat possible, if not serving immediately, to keep warm.

Heat a large nonstick sauté pan over high heat. When the pan is almost smoking, add 1 tablespoon oil. Working in batches, spoon ¼-cup scoops of batter into the skillet, making sure the scoops are about 1 inch apart, and cook on one side until golden brown, about 3 minutes. Flip and cook until the second side is golden brown and the crumpets are cooked through, about 3 minutes more. Repeat with the remaining crumpet batter.

Serve the crumpets warm with the syrup and blueberries.

CRUMPETS

¾ cup whole milk, warmed

1 tablespoon olive oil

1½ teaspoons sugar

1 tablespoon plus 1½ teaspoons active dry yeast

1⅓ cups all-purpose flour

1 cup bread flour

1 tablespoon kosher salt

¼ teaspoon baking soda

CHORIZO MAPLE SYRUP

1 tablespoon canola oil

8 ounces fresh chorizo sausage, any casings removed

1 teaspoon Dijon mustard

1 teaspoon soy sauce

2 cups maple syrup

Canola oil

½ pint blueberries

TIP

Note that in Chinese cooking, "light" soy sauce just means regular ol' soy sauce (*not* low-cal or low-sodium). "Dark" refers to soy sauce that's been reduced so it's thicker and sweeter. You can find dark soy sauce in Asian markets and some grocery stores.

SOURDOUGH BATTER

½ cup sourdough starter (store-bought is fine)

1 large egg

½ tablespoon unsalted butter, melted

½ tablespoon turbinado sugar

1 teaspoon vanilla extract

½ teaspoon baking soda

½ teaspoon kosher salt

BUTTERMILK BATTER

2 large eggs

1¼ cups buttermilk

3 tablespoons canola oil

1½ cups all-purpose flour

3 tablespoons sugar

½ tablespoon baking powder

½ tablespoon baking soda

Unsalted butter, for the griddle

FILLING AND TOPPINGS

Filling of your choice (recipes follow)

Butter of your choice (recipes follow) or unsalted butter

Topping of your choice (recipes follow)

Maple syrup

When I first opened Little Goat, I flipped pancakes on the line for seven days a week. I almost had a mental breakdown because we sell a ton of pancakes! I'm not surprised people are so fond of our pancakes—they're really, really good. They combine the fluffiness of a buttermilk pancake with the savory funkiness of a sourdough one—we literally mix the two batters together.

I change our pancake toppings seasonally. In the fall, I sauté apples in garam masala, a warm and aromatic Indian-inspired spice blend, to give them a little kick and top them with buttermilk butter and an oatmeal crumble—like a giant apple muffin-pie-cake thing. In the summer, blueberries get the same treatment. And whenever I'm feeling a little frisky, there's a chocolate pancake that we serve with chocolate-coated rice crispies baked inside for a surprising crunch, and chocolate butter slathered over the top.

After this basic recipe, I've included two of these variations: Apple and Oat Streusel with Buttermilk Butter, and Chocolate Crispies with Chocolate Malt Butter. Make the fillings and toppings in advance so they are ready to be added to the pancakes as you cook them. *Makes 12 pancakes*

PERFECT PANCAKES, TWO WAYS

Make the sourdough batter:
In a medium bowl, whisk together the starter, egg, butter, turbinado sugar, vanilla, baking soda, and salt.

Make the buttermilk batter:
In a medium bowl, whisk the eggs with the buttermilk and oil. In a large bowl, combine the flour, sugar, baking powder, and baking soda. Form a well in the center of the dry ingredients. Pour the wet ingredients into the well and gently whisk until the batter comes together and there are no lumps. Be careful not to over-mix.

Mix together the buttermilk and sourdough batters. Heat a flat-top griddle or large nonstick sauté pan over medium heat and brush with butter. For each pancake, scoop ⅓ cup of the batter

(Continues)

directly onto the surface (leave 4 inches between each pancake) and cook for 1 minute.

Fill and finish the pancakes:

Add some of your filling of choice. Cook until the edges turn golden brown, about 4 minutes. Flip the pancake, reduce the heat, and cook for another 2 minutes. Repeat with the remaining batter and remaining filling.

Garnish the finished pancakes with a dollop of butter, a sprinkle of your topping of choice, and the maple syrup. Serve hot.

Apple and Oat Streusel with Buttermilk Butter

SAUTÉED APPLE FILLING

4 tablespoons (½ stick) unsalted butter

3 Granny Smith apples, peeled, cored, and thinly sliced

2 teaspoons garam masala

2 tablespoons sugar

In a large sauté pan over medium-high heat, melt 2 tablespoons of the butter. Add half the apple slices and toss to coat. Brown for 2 minutes, then toss again. Cook for another 2 minutes. Season with 1 teaspoon of the garam masala and 1 tablespoon of the sugar. Toss to coat and make sure the apples are tender. Transfer to a sheet tray to cool and repeat with the remaining ingredients.

OAT STREUSEL TOPPING

⅓ cup all-purpose flour

⅔ cup old-fashioned oats

3 tablespoons light brown sugar

⅛ teaspoon ground cinnamon

⅛ teaspoon baking soda

5 tablespoons salted butter

Preheat the oven to 325°F. In the bowl of a stand mixer fitted with the paddle attachment or in a large bowl with a hand mixer or spoon, mix the flour, oats, brown sugar, cinnamon, baking soda, and butter until fully incorporated. Crumble the mixture onto a large sheet tray and bake until golden brown and fluffy, about 15 minutes. Let cool completely. Store in an airtight container at room temperature for up to 1 week.

BUTTERMILK BUTTER

8 tablespoons (1 stick) salted butter, at room temperature

1 tablespoon buttermilk

1 tablespoon sweetened condensed milk

⅛ teaspoon garam masala

In a stand mixer fitted with the paddle attachment, beat the butter until light, about 2 minutes. Add the buttermilk, condensed milk, and garam masala. Mix until well combined. Refrigerate until ready to use.

Chocolate Crispies with Chocolate Malt Butter

CHOCOLATE CRISPIES FILLING AND TOPPING

⅓ cup semi-sweet chocolate chips

2 cups crisp rice cereal

Melt the chocolate chips in a double boiler over hot water or in the microwave in 10-second pulses. Toss the rice cereal in the chocolate until evenly coated and the chocolate is set. Continue tossing consistently while the chocolate sets—this will keep the puffs from sticking together. Store in an airtight container at room temperature for up to 1 week.

CHOCOLATE MALT BUTTER

8 tablespoons (1 stick) salted butter

2 tablespoons sweetened condensed milk

1 teaspoon barley malt syrup

2 teaspoons unsweetened cocoa powder

1 teaspoon malt powder

In the bowl of a stand mixer fitted with the paddle attachment or in a medium bowl with a hand mixer, beat the butter, condensed milk, and barley malt syrup until light and fluffy, about 2 minutes. Add the cocoa powder and malt, and mix until well incorporated. Store in the refrigerator until ready to serve.

These biscuits are enormous—flaky and savory, just like biscuits should be—but it's the gravy that's truly special. When I first put this on the menu, I had no idea how to make sausage gravy, so I used my Thanksgiving green bean casserole gravy as inspiration. I remember making it when I'd just graduated from culinary school and was all gung-ho about cooking everything from scratch. (My mom later told me that she had bought cans of gravy because she wasn't sure mine would turn out, but it ended up being pretty good—one of the first things I got really excited about cooking.) The way I do it now is a little different: I use sausage fat in addition to butter to make a roux and add a pinch of garam masala, which makes your house smell like Thanksgiving-appropriate baking spices while also adding subtle heat. *Serves 6*

BISCUITS

WITH SAUSAGE AND MUSHROOM GRAVY

Make the biscuits:

In a large bowl, whisk together the flour, salt, baking powder, baking soda, and sugar. Cut in the cold butter until the mixture is gritty and sandy in texture. Put the bowl in the freezer for 30 minutes.

Stir the buttermilk into the dough until well combined. Form the dough into a square, wrap in plastic, and refrigerate for 15 minutes. Line a cookie sheet with parchment paper and grease with cooking spray. Roll the dough into a 2-inch-thick square—it doesn't have to be perfectly even. Cut the dough into 6 equal squares. Transfer the biscuits to the cookie sheet and to the freezer for 30 minutes. (Once firm, these can be wrapped in plastic wrap and stored in the freezer for up to a month. You can bake them straight from the freezer; just add 5 minutes to the baking time.)

Preheat the oven to 425°F.

Brush the 2 tablespoons melted butter over the biscuits. Bake the biscuits until they are golden brown and feel firm when gently pressed, 15 to 17 minutes. If they still feel soft, bake for another 5 minutes.

(Continues)

BISCUITS

2 cups all-purpose flour

1½ teaspoons kosher salt

2 tablespoons baking powder

1 teaspoon baking soda

1½ tablespoons sugar

8 tablespoons (1 stick) unsalted butter, cold and cubed, plus 2 tablespoons, melted

1 cup buttermilk

Nonstick cooking spray

GRAVY

3½ cups whole milk

8 ounces mild pork sausage, casings removed

½ cup diced Spanish onion

1 small garlic clove, minced

2 cups sliced cremini mushrooms

5 tablespoons unsalted butter

½ cup all-purpose flour

2 teaspoons kosher salt

½ teaspoon garam masala

¼ cup thinly sliced scallions, white and green parts (optional)

Make the gravy:

In a medium saucepan over low heat, gently warm the milk.

In a medium pot over medium heat, brown the sausage, breaking it up with a wooden spoon as it cooks, 10 minutes. Without draining off any fat, add the onion and garlic, and cook until tender, 5 minutes. Add the mushrooms and cook until tender, 5 minutes.

Stir in the butter and allow it to melt, then whisk in the flour until it's fully incorporated. Cook for 2 minutes before whisking in the warm milk, until fully combined. Reduce the heat to low and allow the gravy to thicken, 15 minutes. Add the salt and garam masala.

Slather the gravy over the biscuits, sprinkle with the scallions (if using), and serve.

Variation: Cheddar-Scallion Biscuits

For a cheesy, slightly Asian twist on this traditional biscuit recipe, add 1 cup shredded cheddar cheese and ½ cup thinly sliced scallions to the dough before adding the buttermilk, but after freezing, then glaze with 4 tablespoons (½ stick) butter melted with 1 teaspoon sesame oil.

SPRING ONION CREAM CHEESE SPREAD

1 tablespoon canola oil

1 cup thinly sliced spring onions (white and green parts)

8 ounces cream cheese, at room temperature

¼ cup shredded MontAmoré (see page 35) or Parmesan cheese

Kosher salt and pepper

CREPES

1½ cups whole milk

1 cup all-purpose flour

3 large eggs

Unsalted butter, for the pan

Nonstick cooking spray

SALAD

3 cups arugula

½ cup shaved fennel bulb

¼ cup drained Pickled Red Onions (page 258), plus ½ cup pickle liquid

¼ cup extra-virgin olive oil

Unsalted butter, for the pan

Crepes are definitely one of those things that freak people out—I mean, they sound fancy and make you think you need a special crepe pan (which you don't). But they're actually super simple; in fact, they were the first dish I made by myself. I was eight years old and we'd just been to Epcot Center and eaten in "France." I really wanted to re-create the ham, cheese, and mushroom crepes we'd had, so I used my mom's cookbooks to figure out how.

Now I like using crepes as a blank canvas for compound cream cheeses for brunch. I love going into a bagel shop and seeing all their fun cream cheese flavors—something you can easily play around with at home. This spring onion version is a favorite, though you could substitute any variation you want, especially if you have leftover smoked salmon cream cheese spread (see page 40).

You can make the crepes the day before you serve them and just brown them in some butter until they're nice and crispy. *Serves 4*

CREPES
WITH SPRING ONION CREAM CHEESE

Make the cream cheese spread:
Heat the oil in a medium pan over medium heat. Add the spring onions and sauté until just tender, about 5 minutes. Set aside to cool.

In a stand mixer fitted with the paddle attachment or in a medium bowl with a hand mixer or spoon, beat the cream cheese for about 1 minute, or until light and fluffy. Stir in the spring onions and cheese, and season with salt and pepper.

Make the crepes:
In a blender, combine the milk, flour, and eggs. Blend until a very smooth batter forms. Heat a small nonstick sauté pan over medium heat. Once it's hot, add a small pat of butter, about ½ tablespoon, and wipe out any excess—the pan should be slick but not greasy. Add just enough batter to coat the bottom of the pan in a thin layer, swirling the pan as you add the batter. Cook until the crepe sets, 2 minutes, then remove it from the pan and transfer to a plate. You do not need to flip the crepe. Continue

(Continues)

BRUNCHING

A little shout-out to my favorite cheese! In our search for local, awesome cheeses to serve in our restaurants, I found this one from the Sartori Cheese Company in Wisconsin. It can hold its own on a cheese plate, and I love to munch on it as is, but it's also a great cooking cheese, whether you're tossing it into salads or adding tanginess to something sweet like ice cream (page 230). It's Parmesan's tangier, creamier cousin, so if you can't find it, you can definitely use a nice Parmesan instead.

making the crepes, buttering the pan as needed. Put a piece of parchment paper that has been sprayed with nonstick cooking spray between each crepe as you complete them. Let the crepes cool completely.

Make the salad:
Toss the arugula, fennel, and pickled onions with the pickle liquid and olive oil.

Spread 2 tablespoons of the cream cheese spread on half of each crepe. Fold the remaining half over the cream cheese filling and fold again to form a triangle. Repeat with all the crepes.

Heat a small, nonstick sauté pan over medium heat. Add a pat of butter and brown both sides of each filled crepe until golden and crispy, about 2 minutes per side. Arrange the browned crepes on a plate and top with the arugula salad.

Almost every South and Central American country has a version of sofrito, a cooked-down mix of vegetables like onions, tomatoes, and sweet peppers that is used to flavor dishes and sauces. I wanted to play with this idea and make the results a little sweeter and more brunchy, so I started with heirloom tomatoes, then added apricots for their acidity and melon for sweetness. I used this sofrito mixture to make a broth with a little chicken stock, threw in a couple poached eggs—whose yolks thicken and richen the sauce—and some crispy bread, and called it brunch. *Serves 4*

POACHED EGGS
WITH TOMATO-MELON-APRICOT SOFRITO

In a large saucepan over medium heat, melt the bacon fat. Add the onions and garlic, and cook until translucent, 3 minutes. Season with the chili powder, pepper, paprika, cinnamon, and a pinch of salt. Add the poblano and bell peppers, and cook until soft, about 10 minutes. Deglaze with the wine and allow the wine to reduce by half, about 2 minutes. Stir in the tomatoes, apricots, and chicken stock and simmer for 1 hour, or until a thick, rich sauce forms. Season the sofrito with the lemon zest and salt to taste.

Fill a large pot with water and bring to a boil. Reduce the heat under the pot of water so that the water simmers and pour in the vinegar.

Pour the sofrito into 4 large, shallow bowls. (You could also refrigerate the sofrito if you're making this ahead. Just reheat before proceeding.)

Crack an egg into a ladle or large spoon and carefully lower it into the simmering water. Use the spoon to keep the egg round as it cooks, about 2 minutes. The white should be opaque and the yolk runny. Transfer the egg so it's fairly nestled in the sofrito, being careful to not break the yolk. Repeat with the remaining eggs. (If you'd like to cook all the eggs at once, you can forgo the shaping process and just crack them into individual bowls, then gently add them to the water one by one. You will lose a bit of the white this way, but they can all be plated at once.)

Garnish the bowls with chiles and mint and serve.

⅓ cup rendered bacon or chicken fat

3 cups thinly sliced sweet onions

1½ tablespoons minced garlic

1 teaspoon chili powder

⅛ teaspoon black pepper

1 teaspoon paprika

¼ teaspoon ground cinnamon

Kosher salt

¾ cup seeded and small-diced poblano chile

1½ cups thinly sliced red bell peppers

1 cup dry white wine

3 cups small-diced ripe heirloom tomatoes

1½ cups small-diced fresh apricots

1½ cups chicken stock

1 teaspoon grated lemon zest

2 tablespoons white vinegar

8 large eggs

Pickled Fresno Chiles (page 263), for serving

Torn mint leaves, for serving

SUNDAY FUNDAY

. . . .

People always think that parties need to be at night, but eating a bunch of yummy food first thing? Sounds great! Or how about doing something different during the holidays? People would be pretty pumped about not having to drag themselves out after work for another night of blah cocktails and passed hors d'oeuvres. Brunch parties have become the new dinner party in our house. We keep things informal and open-house–style. People eat, hang out, mill around, and eat some more. I serve dishes that can just sit there—like Smoked Salmon Toast (page 40) or Razzle Home Fries (page 42), which taste great at pretty much any temperature. I also like a spread to be interactive, so I offer a couple of compound butters or jams and make it a "Choose Your Own Adventure" for how to top scones. All these dishes can be made ahead, which will leave you with plenty of time to hang out and enjoy a Bloody Mary (or two).

- 1 tablespoon canola oil
- ½ cup sliced spring onions (white and green parts)
- 12 large eggs
- ¾ cup heavy cream
- ½ teaspoon kosher salt
- 1½ cups chopped Grilled Pork Belly (page 131) or cooked bacon
- 2 tablespoons unsalted butter
- ¾ cup whole-milk ricotta
- 2 cups bread cubes, from leftover bread, in 1-inch cubes
- Kosher salt
- Pickled Red Onions (page 258), drained, for serving
- ¼ cup assorted fresh herbs, for serving

Cooking eggs doesn't have to be a pain in the ass. When I opened Little Goat, I rediscovered my love of frittatas—which are just eggs beaten together with a little cream and whatever else you can find in your fridge, and baked in the oven. Pretty hard to mess up. They're delicious at room temperature and great for setting out—still in the pan—on a buffet. My one rule is that I never make anything expressly to put in a frittata; I rely solely on leftovers. In this case, I go for Grilled Pork Belly (page 131), ricotta, and spring onions, and I top it with some day-old bread toasted in butter for texture. So, feel free to get creative and clean out that fridge! And try to buy some good local eggs, if you can. Have you ever compared the yolk of a farm egg to a regular grocery-store egg? One is pale yellow, the other bright orange. Guess which one will taste better? *Serves 4*

PORK BELLY FRITTATA

Preheat the oven to 325°F.

In a small pan, heat the oil over medium heat. Add the spring onions and sauté until just soft, about 4 minutes. Remove from the pan and set aside to cool.

In a medium bowl, whisk together the eggs, cream, and salt. Add the pork belly and spring onions, and mix until combined.

Use 1 tablespoon of the butter to grease an ovenproof, round nonstick pan that's at least 6 inches wide at the very bottom. Pour in the egg mixture and top with dollops of ricotta. Bake until the frittata has at least doubled in size and the center doesn't wobble when agitated, about 25 minutes.

Meanwhile, melt the remaining butter in a sauté pan over medium-low heat. Add the bread cubes, toss to coat, add a pinch of salt, and cook the pieces for several minutes on each side until golden brown. Allow to cool.

Top the frittata with pickled onions, herbs, and crusty croutons.

I'm a big fan of smoked salmon and bagel plates, so I wanted to create a more composed version that works as a really light summer dish. I slice a baguette into long pieces, schmear the pieces with cream cheese that's been whipped with little smoked salmon bits, and top off with fresh salmon that we pick into pieces instead of slicing. Then I drizzle on top a simple chile-lime vinaigrette with sambal oelek (a spicy Asian condiment that you can find in most grocery stores these days) and fish sauce for a salty-tangy-spicy mashup and finish everything with crispy fried capers. *Serves 4*

SMOKED SALMON TOAST
WITH CHILE-LIME VINAIGRETTE

Mix the cream cheese spread:
In a stand mixer fitted with the paddle attachment or in a large bowl with a spoon, mix the cream cheese until smooth. Add the smoked salmon in small pieces and incorporate well. Season to taste with salt and pepper.

Make the vinaigrette:
Whisk together the lime juice, oil, fish sauce, and sambal oelek in a medium bowl and season to taste with salt.

Season the fresh salmon on both sides with salt and pepper. Heat the oil in a large nonstick sauté pan over medium heat and cook, turning once, to medium well, 6 minutes per side. Set aside to cool before removing the skin.

Slice the bread on the bias into 1-inch-thick slices. Butter both sides of each slice and toast in a pan over medium heat until golden brown and crunchy, 4 minutes per side. Allow to cool for a few minutes.

Schmear one side of the bread slices with the smoked salmon cream cheese. Break apart the cooked salmon with your fingers into small chunks. Scatter the pieces on top of the cream cheese.

In a medium bowl, toss the arugula, fennel, mint, sorrel, and blackberries with a splash of the chile-lime vinaigrette. Top the salmon with the dressed salad and serve.

SMOKED SALMON CREAM CHEESE SPREAD

1 pound cream cheese, at room temperature

4 ounces good-quality thinly sliced smoked salmon

Kosher salt and pepper

CHILE-LIME VINAIGRETTE

¼ cup fresh lime juice

2 tablespoons canola oil

1 tablespoon fish sauce

½ tablespoon sambal oelek

Kosher salt

1 pound fresh salmon fillet

Kosher salt and pepper

1 tablespoon canola oil

1 baguette

4 tablespoons (½ stick) unsalted butter, at room temperature

3 cups arugula

½ cup shaved fennel bulb

1 tablespoon roughly chopped fresh mint

1 tablespoon roughly chopped fresh sorrel

¾ cup blackberries, quartered

I love home fries, but so often when you go out for brunch it seems like they've been fried three times, all shriveled and crunchy with no actual soft potato left. We've perfected the process so you end up with a nice, creamy inside but lots of great little almost-burnt bits on the outside, too. I use Kennebec potatoes because they're the perfect mix of a Yukon Gold and a russet—not too dry, but not too waxy—and I boil them whole so they don't get waterlogged. Then I break them into pieces instead of dicing them, partly because it looks so much more fun on the plate, but also so you get some of those great crispy nuggets when you fry everything up in a ton of butter. The finishing touch is a dusting of our favorite spice mix. If you're making these for a brunch party, you could cook and crumble the potatoes ahead of time so you don't have to wake up at 6 a.m. to prep.

Serves 4 to 6

Kosher salt

2 pounds medium Kennebec potatoes

8 tablespoons (1 stick) unsalted butter

2 tablespoons Razzle Spice Mix (recipe follows)

¼ cup thinly sliced scallions (white and green parts)

RAZZLE HOME FRIES

Fill a large pot with water and add a healthy pinch of salt. Add the potatoes and bring to a boil. Reduce the heat so that the water is at a low boil. Cook until the potatoes are just fork-tender but not mushy, about 30 minutes. Drain the potatoes and let them cool. Break them up into large, messy chunks.

Heat a large nonstick sauté pan over medium heat. Add half the butter and the broken potato pieces. Sprinkle with the spice mix and 1 tablespoon salt and toss to coat. Allow the potatoes to brown on one side for at least 5 minutes before tossing again. Add the remaining butter and continue to brown the potatoes on all sides. When the potatoes are browned and crispy, after 8 to 10 minutes total, transfer them to a plate and garnish with the scallions.

Razzle Spice Mix

Short for *ras el hanout*, this play on a traditional North African spice mix is just as good on savory foods as it is on sweet.

Makes 2 cups

SPICES TO TOAST

½ cup coriander seeds

3 tablespoons fennel seeds

2 tablespoons cumin seeds

4 teaspoons dried orange rind

1 tablespoon dried lemon rind

3½ teaspoons caraway seeds

1 large cinnamon stick

2 teaspoons cardamom seeds

3¼ teaspoons pink peppercorns

1 tablespoon allspice berries

5 Thai long peppercorns

5 whole star anise

1 teaspoon ground Thai chile

1 dried chile de árbol

12 whole cloves

ADDITIONAL SPICES

2½ tablespoons ground sumac

2¼ teaspoons dried garlic

5¾ teaspoons grated nutmeg

3 tablespoons hibiscus flowers

1 tablespoon mustard seeds

2 teaspoons ground ginger

Combine the spices to toast in a sauté pan over medium-low heat. Toss the spices regularly to ensure even toasting and cook until fragrant, 5 minutes. Let cool completely.

Combine the toasted spices and additional spices in a mortar and pestle or spice grinder and grind finely. Store in an airtight container in the freezer for up to 1 month.

SCONES OF ALL SORTS

Basic Scone Recipe

I always thought scones were kind of dry and dense, and generally boring. But they're a brunch staple, so I wanted to figure out how to make a moist, cakey upgrade that I could put on the menu at the diner. The result is this cross between a scone and a muffin because it's fluffy on the inside yet crackly and crunchy on the outside. So, it turns out I *do* love scones! With one basic recipe, you can mix in all kinds of ingredient combos!

Makes 9 scones

4 cups all-purpose flour

¾ cup granulated sugar

1 tablespoon baking powder

½ tablespoon kosher salt

Scone add-ins (recipes follow)

1 cup (2 sticks) unsalted butter, cold and cubed, plus more for the pan

⅔ cup plus ¼ cup heavy cream

¾ cup fresh orange juice

2 tablespoons turbinado sugar

Combine the flour, granulated sugar, baking powder, salt, and any add-ins. Cut the butter cubes into the dry ingredients, as if you were making a pie crust. The butter should resemble cornmeal when it is thoroughly combined.

In a medium bowl, whisk together ⅔ cup of the heavy cream and the orange juice. Add half the cream mixture to the dry mix and begin to work it into the dough with a spoon. Slowly add more cream mixture until the dough just begins to come together. It should remain slightly dry and crumbly, and not reach the point of being sticky.

Grease a rimmed 9 by 9-inch baking pan and line it with parchment paper. Press the scone dough into the pan so that it fills completely. Cut it into 9 (3 by 3-inch) pieces. Refrigerate for 1 hour.

Preheat the oven to 350°F. Line a baking sheet with parchment paper and place the dough pieces on it 3 inches apart.

Brush the scones with the remaining ¼ cup heavy cream and sprinkle with the turbinado sugar. Bake until golden brown and firm, 20 to 25 minutes. Serve warm or at room temperature. (The raw dough can be stored in the refrigerator for up to 1 week or frozen for up to 1 month. Bake the scones the day you plan to serve them.)

Scone Add-ins

LEMON CHOCOLATE

1 tablespoon grated lemon zest

¾ cup cacao nibs

ROSEMARY DULCE

1 cup white chocolate dulce de leche chips (store-bought is fine)

1 teaspoon roughly chopped fresh rosemary

APRICOT GINGER

⅔ cup chopped dried apricots

1 teaspoon ground ginger

CRANBERRY PEPITA

⅔ cup dried cranberries

½ cup semi-sweet chocolate chips

½ cup unsalted pepitas, toasted

BLUEBERRY FENNEL

1 cup dried blueberries

2 tablespoons fennel seeds

THESE ARE
MY JAMS

You can, of course, make a simple quick jam from whatever perfectly ripe stone fruits you have on hand or berries that are a little too soft for salads—and it would be completely delicious. But I say, have fun with jams! I like to try unexpected combinations, especially by adding savory elements such as herbs and spices. These favorites of mine are the perfect toppers for toast, scones, and muffins.

Blueberry-Tomatillo Jam

My neighbor, who has a house in Michigan, drops off a giant tub of the most amazing, freshly picked blueberries for me every summer. It's more blueberries than two humans could possibly eat by the handful, so I always turn some into a tasty jam. I add some tomatillos to bring a little acidity to the party and a little bit of heat with Korean chile flakes, which aren't as intense as their red pepper flake cousins. *Makes 1½ cups*

1 pint blueberries

1½ pounds tomatillos, husked, rinsed, and cut into quarters

1½ teaspoons crushed red pepper flakes, preferably Korean, or to taste

2 cups sugar

Grated zest and juice of 2 limes

Combine the blueberries, tomatillos, red pepper flakes, sugar, and lime zest and juice in a large nonreactive saucepan. Bring the mixture to a boil over high heat, reduce the heat to medium, and simmer briskly, stirring regularly, until thickened, 30 minutes. Let cool, then transfer to a lidded container, and refrigerate for up to 2 weeks.

Apricot-Pepper Jam

Tart-sweet apricots bring out sweet peppers' sweet side and the dry rosé makes a fun alternative to lemon juice for a little extra acid. *Makes 1½ cups*

2 pounds apricots, pulled in half and pitted

3 Ancient Sweet peppers or other small red bell peppers (about ½ pound), seeded and thinly sliced

2 cups sugar

½ cup dry rosé wine

Combine the apricots, peppers, sugar, and wine in a large nonreactive saucepan. Bring the mixture to a boil over high heat, reduce the heat to medium, and simmer briskly, stirring regularly, until the apricots and peppers are broken down, 30 minutes. Let cool, then transfer to a lidded container, and refrigerate for up to 2 weeks.

Strawberry-Sumac Jam

Sumac has a subtle tart flavor that brings out the sweetness of strawberries. The pale ale adds earthy notes from the hops and another layer of sweetness from the grains. *Makes 1½ cups*

2 pounds strawberries, hulled and quartered

2 cups sugar

½ cup pale ale

1 teaspoon ground sumac

1 teaspoon kosher salt

Combine the strawberries, sugar, ale, sumac, and salt in a large nonreactive saucepan. Bring the mixture to a boil over high heat, reduce the heat to medium, and simmer briskly, stirring regularly, until the strawberries are broken down and saucy, 30 minutes. Let cool, then transfer to a lidded container, and refrigerate for up to 2 weeks.

2 cups sweetened
condensed milk

1 cup half-and-half

This is inspired by Vietnamese coffee, which in addition to totally knocking you on your butt because it's so strong, is seriously sweet and addictive. I wanted to get that flavor in my iced coffee, but you can't just put a lot of sugar in there because it'll never dissolve. And if you try adding simple syrup and cream, it's just too much liquid. What I discovered is that if you combine warmed half-and-half and sweetened condensed milk, you end up with the right milk-sugar ratio and get the most amazing subtle caramel flavor. Make a batch to stash in your fridge and use it as you would regular cream and sugar in your coffee or cereal. *Makes 3 cups*

SWEET CREAM

In a small saucepan over low heat, combine the condensed milk and ½ cup of the half-and-half. Stir until the milk has dissolved, and then remove the mixture from the heat.

Whisk in the remaining half-and-half. Let the mixture cool and then cover and refrigerate for up to a week.

I like a Bloody Mary that has great pickle flavor, which I get courtesy of pickled red onion juice. Add some hot sauce, horseradish, garlic powder, and salt and pepper, and you end up with a mix that's refreshing, isn't too in-your-face spicy, and as good virgin as it is with vodka or gin. And definitely don't forget the blue cheese–stuffed olives. *Makes 10 drinks*

BLOODY MARYS
WITH BLUE CHEESE–STUFFED OLIVES

Stuff the olives:

In a stand mixer with the paddle attachment or in a medium bowl with a hand mixer or spoon, beat the cream cheese until softened. Add the blue cheese and mix until fully incorporated and almost smooth. Transfer the mixture to a piping bag or a large plastic baggie with a corner snipped. Fill each olive with as much cream cheese as it can hold. Refrigerate the olives until ready to serve.

Make the Bloody Mary mix:

In a large pitcher, whisk together the tomato juice, hot sauce, Kimchi Sauce, Worcestershire sauce, miso, pickle liquid, salt, garlic powder, garam masala, and pepper.

To serve individually, combine ½ cup of the mix with 2 ounces vodka or gin over ice cubes, or with 2 tablespoons water for a virgin version. To serve a big batch, place the mix in a pitcher, have the liquor alongside, and offer plenty of ice cubes. Garnish the drinks with the stuffed olives and pickled chiles, if using.

STUFFED OLIVES

4 ounces cream cheese, at room temperature

1 ounce quality blue cheese

10 large green olives, pitted

BLOODY MARY

1 (46-ounce) can quality tomato juice

⅓ cup smoky hot sauce

⅓ cup Kimchi Sauce (page 259)

¼ cup Worcestershire sauce

1 tablespoon white miso paste

3 tablespoons liquid from Pickled Red Onions (page 258)

2½ teaspoons kosher salt

1½ teaspoons garlic powder

1 teaspoon garam masala

1 teaspoon freshly ground black pepper

20 ounces quality vodka or gin

Pickled chiles, for serving (optional)

GIRL & THE GRILL

SHRIMP COCKTAIL
with Miso Blue Sauce................. 55

QUAIL "WINGS"
with Yuzu-Harissa Sauce 56

GRILLED DUCK HEARTS
with Sesame-Horsey Mayo 61

SMOKY BROCCOLI
with Blue Cheese Dressing and
Spiced Krispies....................... 62

GRILLED BOK CHOY SALAD
with Cashew Vinaigrette.............. 64

**HOISIN-GRILLED
SKIRT STEAKS**
with Grilled Pineapple and
Blueberry Pico........................ 65

LAMB RIBS
with Strawberry–White Asparagus
Tapenade............................. 68

KALBI BEEF RIBS
with Spiced and Buttered Coblettes 71

GRILLED CONFIT DUCK LEGS
with Nectarine Kimchi................ 74

GRILLED BABY CARROTS
with Carrot-Top Chimichurri 77

**GRILLED MAITAKE
MUSHROOMS**
with Tart Plums 79

*Fourth of July
Grill-Out*

———

Un-Belize-able Chicken 82

Grilled Potato Salad
with Grilled Scallion
Vinaigrette 85

Bánh Mì Burger 88

Chocolate Peanut
Butter–Covered Cheez-It
S'mores 91

WHEN GARY AND I MOVED INTO OUR HOUSE, ONE OF THE FIRST THINGS we did was have a wood-fire grill installed. There's really nothing better than sitting in the backyard, playing cards, and waiting while something tasty is cooking. I love how wood adds an extra layer of flavor to whatever you're making, whether it's a big, fatty steak or a bunch of fresh veggies.

The grill also gives me a chance to play around with marinades, which are the perfect way to let meat or vegetables soak up even more sweet-salty-acidic-umami goodness, while also making them nice and tender. Unlike traditional marinades, which usually call for a much longer soak, the versions in this section require only a quick dip—maybe 30 seconds to a minute—before heading to the grill. And most of them have some natural sweetness to them, which is enough sugar to caramelize whatever you're grilling, but not enough to burn. These recipes also highlight my favorite trick ever, which is using whatever marinade hasn't been hanging out with your raw proteins and mixing it with mayo to make a creamy sauce or dressing.

Almost all the recipes in this chapter were made on our home grill. That said, you can make this food on whatever grill you have. If you have a charcoal grill, try using woodchip-style briquettes or sprinkle some woodchips on top of the charcoals for extra woodsy, smoky flavor (or pop 'em in the smoker box of your gas grill, if it has one). Feel free to play around with the kind of wood you use, too. There's less aggressive peach wood (which Gary likes the most) or more pungent cherry or hickory.

Whichever kind of grill you're using, make sure you get to know it. Wood and charcoal grills, unlike gas, can have flare-ups that are caused by fat dripping onto the coals from the food. Since many of the recipes in this book call for food to be coated in oil or a marinade before grilling, be mindful that flare-ups can happen. I recommend putting down one piece of whatever you're cooking first to see how the grill responds. Once you feel comfortable, add the rest of the food. If something does happen to catch on fire, just pull it off and move it to a less hot spot. This tester method is a good way to go for any grill, since each one is different. Plus, there are hot spots and cold spots on any grill—it just depends on the grill itself. Whenever I'm cooking in a new kitchen, I always use this method before committing everything to the fire. You never know!

SHRIMP

1½ cups canola oil

3 tablespoons sambal oelek

1 tablespoon minced garlic

1 pound extra jumbo
(16/20 count) peeled
and deveined shrimp,
preferably with tails on

DIPPING SAUCE

1 large egg yolk

2 tablespoons red wine
vinegar

2 tablespoons fresh
lime juice

1 tablespoon Dijon mustard

1 tablespoon Shaoxing
rice wine

1 tablespoon white miso

½ tablespoon soy sauce

½ tablespoon harissa,
homemade (page 58) or
store-bought

2 ounces quality blue
cheese

1 cup canola oil

Kosher salt

When you hear "shrimp cocktail," you probably think of those big trays from Costco. But this is a totally different version—grilled and served with an addictive dipping sauce—that I hope you'll find is better in many ways! (Not to mention cheaper, too.) Just throw together a simple marinade with sambal oelek, garlic, and oil and let the shrimp sit in there for a quick dip, or even overnight if you want to get it done ahead of time. Then all the shrimp need is a couple of minutes per side on the grill.

Miso blue is a dipping sauce I invented after combining miso with blue cheese—basically two of the saltiest, most savory flavors I could think of. The result is an aioli that, once you dip that first shrimp, you'll want to dip everything else into as well. *Serves 6 to 8 as an appetizer*

SHRIMP COCKTAIL
WITH MISO BLUE SAUCE

Marinate the shrimp:
In a small bowl, whisk together the canola oil, sambal oelek, and garlic. Add the shrimp and toss to coat. Let marinate for at least 30 minutes.

Meanwhile, make the dipping sauce:
In a blender, combine the egg yolk, vinegar, lime juice, mustard, rice wine, miso, soy sauce, harissa, and blue cheese. Blend just to combine. With the blender running, drizzle in the oil. Continue blending until the dressing emulsifies and thickens. Season with salt.

Heat a grill or grill pan to medium-high heat and grill the shrimp for 2 to 3 minutes per side. The shrimp will turn a bright orange color when fully cooked. Serve with the miso blue dipping sauce.

When I was working at Jean-Georges's Vong, we would use a sweet soy-based marinade for the quail, and I really liked how it made this sticky, sweet, caramelized, but sort of charred coating on the meat. I came up with my own version, and now I just call it our "quail marinade," even though it gets used for all kinds of things, like chicken or even goat hearts. You can definitely cook the quail in a pan on the stove, but the grill will take it to next-level caramelization. Then stack these babies on a plate and let people eat them like chicken wings.

Yuzu-harissa sauce is a great staple that you can store in the fridge and use just like hot sauce—for finishing soups, in dressings, you get the idea. Harissa is a North African spice blend that by itself is pretty intense, so I temper it with a little brown sugar and a squeeze of yuzu, a tiny Japanese citrus fruit. You can find these at specialty markets or Asian grocery stores, but if you can't find them, use a regular lime instead. *Serves 6 as a starter or 4 as a main course*

QUAIL "WINGS"
WITH YUZU-HARISSA SAUCE

Make the marinade:
Combine the ingredients in a blender and buzz until fully blended.

Make the sauce:
Whisk together the ingredients until well blended.

Prep the quail:
Lay a quail flat on a cutting board. Using your index finger, find the separation between the breasts and form a small indentation to use as a marker. Use a sharp knife to carefully slice the quail in half between the breasts. Then slice off the wing tip at the first joint and discard. Open the halved quail so the flesh is flat to the cutting board. Repeat for the other birds.

Preheat a grill or grill pan to medium heat.

Lay the quail in an even layer in a large shallow baking dish and pour the marinade over the top. Rub the marinade on the birds to coat and let them sit for 10 minutes.

MARINADE
⅔ cup soy sauce

⅓ cup sweet dark soy sauce

¼ cup rice wine vinegar

3 tablespoons extra-virgin olive oil

3 tablespoons Dijon mustard

2 tablespoons sliced shallots

1½ tablespoons chopped fresh ginger

1 garlic clove

1 tablespoon torn fresh mint leaves

1 tablespoon palm sugar, softened or grated, or light brown sugar

½ tablespoon garam masala

½ teaspoon sambal oelek

SAUCE
1 tablespoon harissa, homemade (recipe folows) or store-bought

2 tablespoons fresh yuzu or lime juice

1 tablespoon dark brown sugar

3 tablespoons extra-virgin olive oil

2½ tablespoons fish sauce

QUAIL
6 semi-boneless quail (1½ to 2 pounds)

Fresh herbs, such as basil, for garnish

(Continues)

GATHER & GRAZE

Grill the quail skin side down until the marinade starts to caramelize, 5 to 7 minutes, then flip and cook until caramelized, another 5 minutes. Transfer them to a plate and drizzle with the yuzu-harissa sauce. Garnish with torn herbs.

Harissa

Makes 2 cups

1 dried chile de árbol, seeded

4 dried ancho chiles, seeded

4 dried guajillo chiles, seeded

1 tablespoon fennel seeds

1 tablespoon coriander seeds

½ tablespoon caraway seeds

2 garlic cloves

⅓ cup canola oil

Kosher salt

Rehydrate the three kinds of chiles in ¾ cup hot water for at least 2 hours. Drain and reserve the chiles and water separately.

Toast the fennel, coriander, and caraway seeds in a dry sauté pan over medium heat until fragrant, about 5 minutes. Once cool, grind the spices.

Put the chiles in a blender or food processor and process until they form a smooth paste. Add the spices, reserved soaking water, garlic, and oil and blend until smooth and emulsified. Lightly season with salt. Cover and keep in the fridge for up to 2 weeks.

PAIRING BEER WITH FOOD

—Gary

I'm a beer guy. I've been drinking and brewing beer since longer than I care to admit. That said, I'm not a big fan of pairing every dish at the restaurants with a specific beer (or any drink, for that matter). Simply put, the things *I* like may not be the same things *you* like. So, instead, when I have a group of people coming over to eat, I like to put together a little buffet-type deal that our guests can work their way through as they eat and figure out what works best for their palates.

In fact, I think of the beer selection as a bit like a cheeseboard. People always say—or at least people who are fancier than I am— that a good cheeseboard should have one blue cheese, one sheep's milk cheese, one cow; some soft and some hard. And offer no more than three to five cheeses or you'll overwhelm your guests. Well, the same can sort of be said of putting together a variety of beers to try with a meal. Nothing fancy, just a few cans or bottles (again, only between three and five different kinds) that I crack open so people can pour a little in their glass, try it, take a bite of food, and try something else.

Beer boils down to two styles: ales and lagers. Ales are generally going to have more spiciness to them and are often described as bright, zesty, floral, fruity, and citrusy. Lagers, on the other hand, usually conjure up words like "earthy," "dry," and "snappy." With me so far? Great. Within those two families are all the other kinds of beers you see lining the walls of your liquor store. On the lager side you have beers like pilsners, and on the ale side you have, well, just about everything else. Each style has a different level of bitterness, sweetness, spice, or zestiness. That's why I pick out a few different varieties to keep things interesting—and to make sure that there's always something tasty to drink with whatever we're eating.

Here are a few rules of thumb for picking out what to serve:

- **Think Ale + Lager.**
  Make sure the families are represented.

- **Start with a Welcome Beer.**
  I like something light and easy to drink that goes with everything, like a kolsch, pale ale, or cider.

- **Try Something Local.**
  I have a lot of love for brew pubs. Explore the options in your own city and embrace the little guys—you're gonna get a good bang for your buck.

- **Add Something Cool, Noteworthy, or Just Plain Weird.**
  Whether it's cans of Pipeworks' Ninja vs. Unicorn (a totally insane Double IPA, which is basically beer on steroids), or one bottle of The Lost Abbey's Red Poppy Ale (a sour cherry–laced brown ale that's aged in oak barrels for over twelve months with very limited release), throw in something that people can talk about.

2 tablespoons fermented black beans, soaked in hot water for 10 minutes and drained

¼ cup bottled prepared horseradish

⅓ cup soy sauce

¼ cup sherry vinegar

2 tablespoons toasted sesame oil

¼ cup canola oil

1 pound duck hearts, halved lengthwise

Kosher salt

1½ cups mayonnaise

Chopped cilantro, to garnish

GOOD STUFF:
FERMENTED BLACK BEANS

These aren't actually black beans but instead are soybeans that have been fermented, a.k.a. salted and dried, at which point they turn black. Once you've soaked them in water for a few minutes to draw out some of the saltiness, they add a sharp salinity to dishes. A little goes a long way, and don't be tempted to just pop one in your mouth right out of the package. They are a bit overwhelming on their own.

First a pep talk: Don't be scared of the hearts! Not only do they have incredible flavor and texture—so meaty!—but they're also so good for you; there are tons of vitamins in that meat. Plus, after a soak in a marinade and a minute or two on the grill, they just taste like sausage. Thread them on skewers and let people drag them through this sesame-horseradish (or "horsey," as I like to call it) mayo, which has a lot of Asian-ish flavor with a nice kick. If you have any aioli left over, it's delicious on a sandwich or eggs, or drizzled over roasted oysters for a fancy-schmancy appetizer.

Serves 6 to 8 as an appetizer

GRILLED DUCK HEARTS
WITH SESAME-HORSEY MAYO

Soak about 20 bamboo skewers in hot water for 1 hour.

Preheat a grill or grill pan to medium-high heat.

In a blender, combine the fermented black beans, horseradish, soy sauce, vinegar, sesame oil, and canola oil and blend until fully incorporated. Reserve ¼ cup and pour the rest into a shallow baking dish.

Skewer the halved hearts lengthwise. Leave the hearts at the top end of each skewer so they will be easier to turn on the grill, 1 halved heart per skewer. Season the hearts with salt and add to the baking dish. Turn to coat in the marinade and let sit for 5 minutes.

Whisk together the reserved ¼ cup marinade and the mayonnaise.

Grill the hearts, turning to cook on all sides, until firm, 5 to 7 minutes. Discard any marinade left in the baking dish.

Spread a thick dollop of the sauce on a plate. Transfer the hot hearts directly from the grill on top of the aioli. Garnish with cilantro and serve immediately.

This is a great make-ahead dish for a barbecue because the broccoli is cooked in advance and the vinaigrette can be stored in the fridge for a few days. So, all you have to do before serving is lightly char the broccoli on the grill and then layer it over chunky smoky blue cheese dressing. People ask all the time if there's bacon in this dish because it has a ton of meaty, smoky, fatty flavor—pretty impressive for broccoli! *Serves 8 to 10*

SMOKY BROCCOLI

WITH BLUE CHEESE DRESSING
AND SPICED KRISPIES

Preheat a grill or grill pan to medium-high heat.

Bring a large pot of heavily salted water to a rolling boil. Prepare a large bowl of ice water. Blanch the broccoli in the boiling water for 4 minutes, scoop it out, and immediately transfer it to the ice bath. Once cool, drain thoroughly.

In a large bowl, whisk together the vinegar, shallots, mustard, soy sauce, Sriracha, harissa, lemon zest, and lemon juice. Whisk quickly as you slowly pour in the olive oil to emulsify the vinaigrette. Reserve 1½ teaspoons for the Spiced Krispies.

Toss the broccoli with the vinaigrette. Grill the broccoli, turning frequently, until the broccoli is evenly charred, about 7 minutes.

Spread the blue cheese dressing onto a serving plate and top with the grilled broccoli. Sprinkle with Spiced Krispies and serve warm.

2 pounds broccoli, cut into large florets

2 tablespoons seasoned rice wine vinegar

2 tablespoons minced shallots

½ tablespoon Dijon mustard

½ tablespoon soy sauce

¾ teaspoon Sriracha hot sauce

¾ teaspoon harissa, homemade (page 58) or store-bought

1 scant teaspoon grated lemon zest

½ tablespoon fresh lemon juice

¼ cup extra-virgin olive oil

Spiced Krispies (page 219, but swap out the garam masala for 1½ teaspoons of the above vinaigrette)

Blue Cheese Dressing (recipe follows)

Blue Cheese Dressing

Makes about ¾ cup

⅓ cup heavy cream

2 heaping tablespoons good blue cheese (I like Rogue Creamery Smokey Blue), plus ¼ cup crumbled

Heaping ¼ teaspoon dark brown sugar

Pinch of kosher salt

Pinch of crushed red pepper flakes

¼ cup sour cream

Combine the cream, 2 tablespoons blue cheese, the brown sugar, salt, and red pepper flakes in a medium saucepan and cook over medium-high heat, stirring, until the cheese is melted. Remove the pot from the heat and fold in the sour cream and remaining ¼ cup crumbled blue cheese. Use immediately, or store in an airtight container, refrigerated, until ready to use—up to 3 days.

This bright, Asian-influenced salad takes bok choy that has been grilled until just tender but still retains the right amount of crunch, and adds salty cashews; funky, salty fish sauce; and sweet pickled shallots. *Serves 4*

GRILLED BOK CHOY SALAD

WITH CASHEW VINAIGRETTE

Preheat a grill or grill pan to medium heat.

In a medium bowl, mix the cashews, shallots and pickle liquid, olives, olive oil, tarragon, fish sauce, and ginger.

Toss the bok choy with the canola oil and season with salt and pepper. Grill, turning once, until tender and lightly browned, 5 to 7 minutes.

Transfer the bok choy to a serving platter, top with the cashew vinaigrette, and serve.

½ cup roasted and salted cashews, roughly chopped

¼ cup Pickled Shallots (page 264), plus 3 tablespoons pickle liquid

¼ cup chopped pitted kalamata olives

2 tablespoons extra-virgin olive oil

1 tablespoon roughly chopped fresh tarragon

1 tablespoon fish sauce

¼ teaspoon finely grated fresh ginger

1 pound baby bok choy, halved lengthwise if small and quartered if larger

2 tablespoons canola oil

Kosher salt and pepper

1 (½-inch-thick) wheel of peeled fresh pineapple

1 cup diced tomatoes

½ cup fresh blueberries

2 tablespoons minced shallot

2 garlic cloves, minced

¼ cup roughly chopped fresh cilantro

2 teaspoons sambal oelek

2 tablespoons extra-virgin olive oil

1 tablespoon fresh lemon juice

STEAK

2 cups quality mayonnaise

2 cups hoisin sauce, homemade (recipe follows) or store-bought

2 to 3 pounds skirt steak

Canola oil

Kosher salt

Skirt steak is basically Gary's favorite thing in the world. If he walks into the kitchen and sees a pile of anything—even lobster—he'll ask hopefully, "Skirt steak?" It's our dog Burt's favorite, too. They both love it so because skirt steak is one of the most flavorful cuts of beef. It's inexpensive—certainly less expensive than the more popular tenderloin—and doesn't require any major cooking other than a quick dip in some marinade and a little time on the grill.

Gary is also obsessed with grilled pineapple. I get it: the sugars caramelize and the fruit gets a little smoky from the grill. I really like tossing it with some tomatoes, red onions, blueberries, and herbs to make a salsa-like condiment that is just as good on steak as it is with Masa Chips (page 167). Add some flour tortillas and it's Taco Night!

I really like making this dish when people come over because it's good at room temp, or even cold, which means you can make it in advance (which is a major stress-reliever).

Serves 6 to 8

HOISIN-GRILLED SKIRT STEAKS
WITH GRILLED PINEAPPLE AND BLUEBERRY PICO

Make the pico:
Preheat a grill or grill pan over medium heat.

Grill the pineapple, turning once, until lightly charred, about 2 minutes per side. Keep the grill fired up for the steaks.

Dice the pineapple and combine in a medium bowl with the tomatoes, blueberries, shallot, garlic, cilantro, sambal oelek, olive oil, and lemon juice. Set aside at room temperature for 30 minutes before serving.

Prepare the steak:
Mix the mayonnaise with 3 tablespoons of the hoisin sauce. Rub the skirt steak with the remaining hoisin sauce and marinate for 5 to 10 minutes.

(Continues)

Hoisin has earned a spot in my pantry and in my heart because it's so much more than just a condiment; it adds another layer of flavor in vinaigrettes, soups, and sauces. It also makes a great marinade, especially because it doesn't take much time for it to impart a lot of flavor to meat. I usually make my own because it's not hard and I can use dates to thicken and sweeten it without a ton of sugar (which can make your meat burn to a crisp instead of just caramelize). Plus, there's nothing better than mixing any leftovers with mayo and slathering it on a breakfast sandwich.

Grill the steak over medium-high heat until medium rare, 3 to 4 minutes on each side. Allow to rest on a cutting board for 10 minutes before slicing against the grain.

Smear a platter with the hoisin mayo and top with the steak and pico.

Hoisin Sauce

Makes 4 cups

¼ cup fermented black beans

4 dates, pitted

2 cups soy sauce

⅔ cup dark soy sauce

¼ cup molasses

4 teaspoons toasted sesame oil

2 garlic cloves, roughly chopped

3 fresh Thai chiles, seeded

Soak the beans and dates in ½ cup warm water for about 10 minutes. Drain, reserving the soaking liquid.

Combine the beans, dates, soy sauces, molasses, sesame oil, garlic, and chiles in a blender and blend until thick and smooth. If the sauce is too thick, add 1 tablespoon of the reserved soaking liquid.

This will keep, covered in the fridge, for up to 1 week.

Everyone knows pork ribs, but lamb ribs, on the other hand, are special because they have a rich flavor with lots of meaty fattiness. Even better, you can pre-cook them in this recipe, then throw them on the grill just to warm them up and get a little smoke. You could also cook these in the oven low and slow until they're nice and tender, and then reheat them under the broiler.

The tapenade is really just a savory fruit salad. I'm not usually nuts about strawberries, but when they get tossed with a fish sauce and red wine vinegar combo (the best ever) and tons of fresh herbs—plus some white asparagus for crunch—it's a whole other story. If you can't find nice strawberries, you could substitute blueberries or halved blackberries. *Serves 6 to 8*

LAMB RIBS
with STRAWBERRY–WHITE ASPARAGUS TAPENADE

Preheat the oven to 325°F.

Prep the ribs:
Season the meat with salt and thoroughly and evenly rub them with the spice mix. Wrap the rib slabs first in plastic wrap and then again in foil. Make sure the sides are well sealed. Lay the ribs flat on a sheet tray and roast for 3 hours. Allow the ribs to cool before unwrapping.

Make the tapenade:
In a large bowl, combine all the ingredients except the strawberries. Add the fruit once you're ready to serve.

Preheat a grill or grill pan to medium heat.

Finish the ribs on the grill—just long enough to get a little smokiness and char, 5 to 7 minutes, turning once. Transfer to a platter and top with the tapenade.

RIBS

3 pounds lamb rib slabs

Kosher salt

Razzle Spice Mix (page 43)

TAPENADE

¾ cup thinly sliced white asparagus (stalks peeled before measuring)

¼ cup thinly sliced spring onions or scallions

2 tablespoons roughly chopped fresh sorrel

2 tablespoons roughly chopped fresh parsley

1 tablespoon roughly chopped fresh cilantro

1 tablespoon roughly chopped fresh basil

¼ cup pitted and roughly chopped Niçoise olives

¼ cup fish sauce

⅓ cup red wine vinegar

½ cup extra-virgin olive oil

1½ cups thinly sliced strawberries or other seasonal berries

1 cup fish sauce

½ cup malt vinegar

¼ cup extra-virgin olive oil

2 tablespoons sambal oelek

2 small garlic cloves, minced

RIBS AND CORN

2 pounds kalbi-style beef short ribs

8 tablespoons (1 stick) unsalted butter, melted

5 ears of sweet corn, cut into 3-inch "coblettes"

Canola oil

Kosher salt

Grilled Okra Relish (recipe follows)

Most people are used to beef short ribs as a big, stewy, hearty dish that's cooked low and slow until the meat is falling off the bone. But Koreans do things a little differently. Kalbi ribs are cooked quick and hot on the grill so they're tender and chewy, meant to be picked up and eaten with your hands. This dish takes that Korean inspiration and mixes it with southern barbecue. If they ate okra in Korea, I'd like to think they'd probably eat it this way, too. The corn on the cob wheels rolled in melted butter that has been mixed with a little of the kalbi marinade then seal the deal. *Serves 6 to 8*

KALBI BEEF RIBS
WITH SPICED AND BUTTERED COBLETTES

Make the marinade:
Combine the fish sauce, vinegar, olive oil, sambal oelek, and garlic in a blender and blend until smooth.

Preheat a grill or grill pan to medium-high heat.

Prepare the ribs and corn:
Arrange the kalbi ribs in a single layer in a baking dish. Pour all but 2 tablespoons of the marinade over the ribs and let them sit for 5 to 10 minutes.

Whip the remaining 2 tablespoons marinade with the melted butter to combine.

Toss the corn coblettes with just enough canola oil to coat and season with salt. Grill, turning once, until tender and just-cooked, about 10 minutes. Dunk the corn in the flavored butter and transfer to a rimmed platter (to catch all the juices).

Grill the ribs for 2 to 3 minutes per side, until you get a nice char. Let the meat cool slightly, then cut between each bone segment so you have 2-inch individual ribs. Plate the ribs on top of the corn coblettes and serve with the remaining flavored butter and the okra relish.

Grilled Okra Relish

Okra is one of those ingredients that gets a bad rap because, when stewed, it can get really gross and goopy. Usually you see it fried or pickled, but grilling it is another awesome way to prepare it. I made this for an event in Nashville, and I could hear the southerners saying, "Grilled okra, oh my!" But if you let the okra get just a little bit of char and then lightly coat it in vinaigrette without stirring too much, it doesn't get sticky.

Makes 2 cups

2 pounds okra	3 tablespoons fish sauce
Canola oil	1 tablespoon malt vinegar
Kosher salt	½ tablespoon minced shallot
1 large poblano chile	

Preheat a grill or grill pan so it's nice and hot.

In a large bowl, toss the okra with just enough oil to coat and a good pinch of salt. Char the okra over high heat, turning once, until it starts to just char and grill marks appear, 1 to 2 minutes, then remove from the heat.

Grill the poblano chile, turning as needed, until the skin is blistering, about 4 minutes per side. Remove from the heat and transfer to a bowl. Cover with plastic wrap and allow to cool for 10 minutes. Remove the skin and seeds.

Slice the okra into ½-inch rounds, discarding the stem ends. Dice the roasted poblano into pieces about the same size as the okra slices.

In a small bowl, whisk together the fish sauce and vinegar. Toss the okra, chile, and shallots together with the dressing. Bring to room temperature before serving and using immediately.

Duck confit—or salted duck legs that have been cooked slowly in fat until juicy, tender, and almost falling apart—is usually prepared in advance and then reheated in the oven. But I like the idea of throwing it on the grill. The fat from the confit drips onto the coals, making the duck nice and smoky. Normally people will let the duck sit in the salt overnight, but I think it can get too salty that way. Instead, I just leave it for an hour. As for the cooking fat, always save your drippings when cooking meat (except for lamb, which has a really strong flavor). Store it in a jar in the fridge—it will last almost forever—and when you have enough, cook some duck legs. You can always round things out with a little bit of oil, if need be. Nectarine kimchi, made from tart, crunchy unripe nectarines, has the perfect bright flavor to cut through the fattiness of the meat. The result is a little spicy, a little salty, and just the right amount of funky. *Serves 4 to 6*

GRILLED CONFIT DUCK LEGS
WITH NECTARINE KIMCHI

Preheat the oven to 300°F.

Make the duck confit:
Rub the duck legs in the salt and let sit for 1 hour. Rinse under cold water and pat dry.

In a wide pot over low heat, combine the duck fat, ginger, garlic, and thyme. Submerge the duck legs in the melted fat. Cover the pot tightly with foil and then the lid. Put in the oven and cook until the meat is tender and shrinks from the bone, 4 to 5 hours.

Uncover the pot and leave the duck submerged in the fat as it cools. Once cool, transfer the duck and fat to a baking dish and refrigerate. (You can store it like this for weeks, if not months.)

Make the nectarine kimchi:
In a medium bowl, toss the nectarine slices with the Kimchi Sauce. Garnish with the fresh herbs.

Preheat a grill or grill pan to medium heat.

Remove the duck from the fat and grill it skin side down until crispy, about 5 minutes. Serve with the nectarine kimchi.

DUCK CONFIT

3 pounds whole duck legs (about 4 legs)

¼ cup kosher salt

8 cups melted duck or meat fat or canola oil

1 (4- to 6-inch) piece fresh ginger, peeled and roughly chopped

6 garlic cloves, peeled

4 sprigs of thyme

NECTARINE KIMCHI

4 unripe nectarines, cut into thin half-moon slices

1 cup Kimchi Sauce (page 259)

2 tablespoons chopped fresh herbs, such as mint or sorrel

TIP

This recipe uses every part of the carrot, so buy baby carrots with the greens still attached. To avoid losing too much of the carrot, do not peel them. Instead, just scrub them with the rough side of a sponge under cold running water.

¼ cup finely chopped
   carrot greens

2 tablespoons minced
   shallots

¼ cup chopped fresh mint

2 tablespoons brine-packed
   capers, roughly chopped

½ cup extra-virgin olive oil

¼ cup red wine vinegar

2 tablespoons soy sauce

1 teaspoon sambal oelek

CARROTS

1½ pounds baby carrots
   (see Tip)

1 tablespoon canola oil

Kosher salt and pepper

I'm always looking for fun new things to grill, especially veggies. When I saw baby carrots at the farmers' market with the greens still attached—not the sad, tiny nubbins at the grocery store—I figured it would be fun to throw 'em onto the fire, then move them to a cooler part of the grill to cook all the way through so they get lots of smoky flavor but are not completely charred. I wanted to use the greens, too, so I blended them with chimichurri-inspired ingredients, like capers, shallots, mint, and olive oil, to make a slightly bitter condiment that complements the sweetness of the carrots.

Serves 4

GRILLED BABY CARROTS
WITH CARROT-TOP CHIMICHURRI

Preheat a grill or grill pan to medium-high heat.

Make the chimichurri:
In a medium bowl, mix the chimichurri ingredients and set aside.

Make the carrots:
In a large bowl, toss the carrots with the canola oil and a pinch of salt and pepper.

Grill the carrots over direct heat, rotating them as they cook, until grill marks form, about 5 minutes. Move the carrots to a cooler part of the grill and continue cooking until the carrots are tender, another 5 minutes.

Transfer the carrots to a serving platter, spoon the chimichurri over the top, and serve.

¼ cup white balsamic vinegar

2 tablespoons honey

4 tablespoons canola oil

1 tart plum, pitted and cut into ¼-inch slices

1 tablespoon minced shallot

2 tablespoons brine-packed capers

¼ cup Pickled Hungarian Hots and Bananas (page 262)

2 tablespoons chopped fresh basil

⅓ cup crumbled blue cheese

4 (4-ounce) packages of maitake mushrooms, quartered

Kosher salt and pepper

The key ingredient for this dish is the plums, so make sure you're getting nice, firm, just-underripe fruit that's more crunchy and tart than sweet and mushy. That's what is going to give you the great texture and nice, bright acidity that pairs so well with salty capers and blue cheese, plus hearty grilled maitakes. I personally would take a grilled maitake over a portobello any day, because they have an even bigger, earthier flavor. They give this dish enough meaty oomph that you don't feel like you're missing out on eating a steak (though the plum salad would be pretty awesome spooned over some just-grilled beef, too . . .). *Serves 4*

GRILLED MAITAKE MUSHROOMS
WITH TART PLUMS

In a medium bowl, mix the vinegar, honey, and 2 tablespoons of the canola oil. Gently fold in the plum, shallot, capers, pickled peppers, and basil. Sprinkle with the blue cheese.

Preheat a grill or grill pan to medium-high heat.

Toss the mushrooms with the remaining 2 tablespoons canola oil and season with salt and pepper. Grill the mushrooms, turning once, until browned on the outside and just tender, 3 minutes per side.

Transfer the mushrooms to a serving platter and top with the plum salad.

FOURTH OF JULY
Grill-Out

....

Since moving into our house, we have really liked having people over for holidays like the Fourth of July. It's a good excuse to see friends and cook a bunch of food. Instead of a more formal sit-down situation, we like to go for something that's more of an all-day eating and drinking extravaganza. The key to that kind of vibe is how you serve the food. If you're not making a ton of food—like the dishes on this menu—then just put things out on a table and let the guests graze. If you're going big and adding a bunch more dishes, then instead of putting the whole spread out at once (which can be overwhelming, for you and your guests) or coursing out your menu (which is a little uptight), just pass things around as they're ready. Put a little bit out, let people eat and try the food with different beers, and then you can send out some more food. It keeps the party going longer, and it gives you a chance to eat and mingle, too.

Gary and I went to Belize for our honeymoon and ended up hanging out with a guide named Javier—who is apparently the only person in Belize who's ever seen a jaguar. We spent a couple days seeing the ruins and, of course, talking about food. Javier said we had to try the Belizean "season all" that they use for their chicken. It's an intense—secret—blend of spices that's a little bit hot and completely delicious. We smuggled out packets of the stuff so that, once home, we could try to re-create it. At the restaurants, we call our version the "un-Belize-able" spice blend. It's a little spicy, a little zesty, and brings grilled chicken to life—though it would also be great on pork chops, grilled fish, or even your Thanksgiving turkey.

The other key to great chicken is brining. It helps keep the meat moist and imparts more flavor than if you just seasoned the outside. You just have to plan ahead so you can give your chicken a good eight-hour soak. (And be careful not to over-brine or you'll end up with chicken that has the weird texture of store-bought turkey lunchmeat.)

I like to slather this juicy, spicy, smoky chicken off the grill with tonkatsu sauce, which is normally served in Japanese restaurants with breaded and fried pork. It's thick, sweet, and salty and is great with about any kind of meat. *Serves 6 to 8*

UN-BELIZE-ABLE CHICKEN

Prepare the chicken:
Combine the salt, sugar, onion, garlic, peppercorns, coriander, and red pepper flakes in a large pot and add 8½ cups water. Bring to a boil and whisk until the sugar and salt are fully dissolved. Remove from the heat and allow the mixture to cool for 15 minutes. Add the ice water to the brine along with the orange and thyme. Stir and allow the brine to cool fully to room temperature. When cool, submerge the chicken in the brine and set in the refrigerator to brine for 8 hours.

Preheat a grill or grill pan to medium heat.

Make the tonkatsu sauce:
Whisk together all the ingredients and set aside.

(Continues)

CHICKEN

1 cup kosher salt

¾ cup granulated sugar

1 medium onion, quartered

2 tablespoons roughly chopped garlic

1 tablespoon black peppercorns

1 teaspoon coriander seeds

¼ teaspoon crushed red pepper flakes

4 cups ice water

1 orange, quartered

1 tablespoon fresh thyme leaves

1 large (3- to 4-pound) chicken or 2 small (2-pound) chickens

TONKATSU SAUCE

2½ cups ketchup

⅓ cup yellow mustard

¼ cup tamarind paste

2 tablespoons Worcestershire sauce

2 tablespoons gochujang chile paste

1½ tablespoons soy sauce

1½ tablespoons fresh lemon juice

½ teaspoon toasted sesame oil

1 tablespoon palm sugar

⅛ teaspoon ground black pepper

⅛ teaspoon ground star anise

¼ teaspoon ground ginger

¼ teaspoon garlic powder

¼ teaspoon onion powder

Un-Belize-able Spice Mix (recipe follows)

Fresh green herbs, such as basil, for garnish

Grill the chicken:

Lay the chicken breast side down. Use poultry shears to cut on either side of the spine and remove it. Press firmly on the split sides to crack the breastbone. Using a sharp knife, split the chicken down the middle of the breastbone. Next, use your fingers to find the separation between the thigh muscle and the bottom of the breast. There should be a small space that's mostly skin in between the pointy bottom of the breast section and the round top of the thigh. Carefully cut around the thigh and remove the whole leg from either side. Then cut the tips of the wings off at the first joint and discard (they tend to burn on the grill). Pat the chicken dry with paper towels and rub all over with the spice rub.

Grill the chicken pieces, turning every 5 minutes, for a total time of 20 to 25 minutes. You'll know it's done when an instant-read thermometer inserted into the thigh (away from a bone) registers 165°F. Remove the chicken from the grill, slather it with tonkatsu sauce, and garnish with the herbs.

Un-Belize-able Spice Mix

Makes 1½ cups

2 dried ancho chiles, toasted	4 teaspoons smoked paprika
4 dried chiles de árbol, toasted	2½ teaspoons annatto seed
2 cinnamon sticks	1 heaping tablespoon black peppercorn
3 tablespoons onion powder	1½ teaspoons coriander seed
2 tablespoons garlic powder	2 teaspoons allspice berries
5½ teaspoons celery seed	2 teaspoons malt powder
4 teaspoons toasted lemon rind	1 teaspoon grated nutmeg

Add the chiles to a small dry skillet over medium heat. Toast until fragrant and lightly browned, 2 to 3 minutes.

In a spice grinder, finely grind all the ingredients to a smooth powder and then blend until well incorporated. Store for 1 month in an airtight container at room temperature, or for longer in the freezer.

I'm always thinking about having the right amount of acidity in a dish. There's something amazing that happens when you add that bright note, almost making all the other flavors taste that much better. Two of my favorite ingredients I use to do that are tamarind and sorrel. Tamarind is a pod that grows mainly in Asia and Africa, but lucky for you, it can be bought as a ready-made paste in most Asian markets (and many regular grocery stores). It's super acidic, but once you add it to things like dressings and marinades, you can taste its natural sweetness. As for sorrel, I keep a plant on our roof because I love it so much. It's an herb that just tastes *fresh*, with the tart acidity of a green apple but none of the sweetness. Use it any time you would other fresh green herbs.

POTATOES

Kosher salt

3 pounds fingerling
potatoes

5 tablespoons unsalted
butter

DRESSING

2 bunches of spring onion
greens or scallions

2½ tablespoons canola oil

Kosher salt

1 tablespoon champagne
vinegar

1 tablespoon white miso

½ tablespoon Dijon mustard

1 teaspoon hot sauce of
your choice

SALAD

4 spring onions (white
bulbs only), quartered

½ pint fresh blueberries

Canola oil

¼ cup fresh mint leaves,
torn

When we finally got a grill—a little gas number—for our first apartment together, Gary made me dinner. He boiled some potatoes and then finished them on the grill. It was a revelation—I'd never thought of doing that before. And it's a good thing I added that into my rotation because the only way to get Gary to eat any veggies is to grill them.

Instead of adding mayo to this potato salad, I toss everything with a grilled scallion-miso dressing. It's a smoky sauce that's also really good with meats like steak and chicken, or on its own as a dipping sauce. *Serves 6 to 8*

GRILLED POTATO SALAD
WITH GRILLED SCALLION VINAIGRETTE

Preheat a grill or grill pan to medium heat.

Boil the potatoes:
Fill a medium pot with room temperature water. Add a handful of salt to the water and then the potatoes. Bring the water to a rolling boil and then reduce the heat so that the water simmers. Cook until the potatoes are just fork-tender, about 15 minutes (they'll finish cooking on the grill). Drain the potatoes, and when cool enough to handle, cut in half lengthwise.

Make the dressing:
Toss the spring onion greens with ½ tablespoon of the oil and season with a pinch of salt. Grill until just charred, turning once, about 2 minutes. Transfer them to a blender or food processor and add the vinegar, miso, mustard, hot sauce, and 3 tablespoons water. Puree until the mixture is bright green and smooth. Add the remaining 2 tablespoons oil and blend on high for 1 more minute. Season to taste with salt.

To finish the potatoes on the grill, you'll need a large piece of aluminum foil, big enough for all the potatoes to fit face-down and still have enough left over to fold up the edges. Put the foil on a sheet pan. Rub a thick layer of butter on the foil, leaving a 2-inch lip around the edges. Put the potatoes on the foil, flesh side down. Dot any remaining butter around the potatoes. Curl the edges of the foil up around the potatoes to help hold the melted butter in place.

(Continues)

Slide the foil and potatoes onto the grill and cook for at least 10 minutes. Check them occasionally to make sure they are browning but not burning. Flip the potatoes once the flesh is golden brown. Allow the skin side to cook for a few minutes before removing from the heat. Transfer the potatoes to a large bowl and toss with a liberal amount of the dressing.

While the potatoes are cooking, drizzle the spring onion bulbs and the blueberries with a little oil and sprinkle with salt. Put the quartered spring onions directly onto the grill (on a spot that isn't super-hot) and cook, turning occasionally, until evenly charred and tender, about 5 minutes. Slice them into bite-size pieces and add them to the bowl with the potatoes.

Use a grill basket or seafood pan to grill the blueberries. The berries will need no more than 2 minutes on the heat. They'll turn a darker blue color when they're done.

Put the dressed potatoes and spring onions on a platter. Top with the grilled blueberries and torn mint. Serve warm or at room temperature.

This is inspired by the bánh mì sandwich, a Vietnamese classic that's basically a bunch of meats with pickled vegetables and a little spice. My secret for perfect burgers is keeping the patty simple—just season it with some salt before it goes on the grill. The best finishing touch is putting the buns on the grill sliced side down so the outside gets a little charred and crisp while the inside stays soft and fluffy. It really does make all the difference. It's worth noting that these burgers are *big*, which makes them perfect for sharing, especially if there's lots of other food on your spread. *Makes 6 burgers*

BÁNH MÌ BURGER

Preheat a grill or grill pan to medium-high heat.

Toss together the pickled carrots, pickled chiles, bean sprouts, and cilantro.

In another bowl, make the spicy mayo by combining the mayonnaise, hot sauce, fish sauce, mustard, and soy sauce.

Form the ground meat into 6 patties, each 1 inch thick. Season with salt and pepper and grill until desired doneness is achieved, about 5 minutes per side for medium rare.

Toast the buns sliced side down over low heat. Spread with the spicy mayo and sandwich each with a burger patty and some crunchy pickle slaw.

⅓ cup Pickled Carrots (page 258)

⅓ cup Pickled Fresno Chiles (page 263)

½ cup mung bean sprouts

¼ cup roughly chopped fresh cilantro

1 cup mayonnaise

¼ cup sweet and spicy hot sauce (habanero varieties work best)

1½ tablespoons fish sauce

1 teaspoon Dijon mustard

½ teaspoon soy sauce

3 pounds 80% lean ground beef

Kosher salt and pepper

6 quality store-bought sesame-seed buns

8 ounces milk chocolate pieces

½ cup creamy peanut butter

3 tablespoons unsalted butter

1 (11.7-ounce) box Cheez-Its Bigs (make sure they're all whole)

½ cup confectioners' sugar

2 tablespoons unsweetened cocoa powder

Marshmallows

When I told Matthew Rice, the former pastry chef at Girl & the Goat, how much I like Cheez-Its, he said we should try coating them with chocolate and peanut butter. Lo and behold, they taste just like little Butterfingers. (He actually made a Cheez-It wedding cake for Gary and me that had them on the inside.) So when I was thinking about things to do on the grill for Fourth of July, I immediately thought of s'mores—and then chocolate and peanut butter–coated Cheez-Its. Let your guests toast their marshmallows over the fire—I've always been into low and slow instead of blackened, but it's a personal decision—then slide them onto a Cheez-It sandwich. It's like a homemade candy bar. *Serves 6 to 8*

CHOCOLATE PEANUT BUTTER—COVERED CHEEZ-IT S'MORES

Bring a few inches of water in a medium saucepan to a boil over medium heat.

Combine the chocolate, peanut butter, and butter in a heatproof bowl that fits over the top of the pot. Melt the ingredients over the boiling water, stirring until combined.

Remove from the heat and add to the Cheez-Its in a bowl. Toss to coat and then let sit for 10 to 15 minutes to avoid clumping when you add the powders.

Combine the confectioners' sugar and cocoa powder. Toss with the coated Cheez-Its.

Toast the marshmallows over the open flame of a grill or stove. Smoosh the melting marshmallow between two coated Cheez-Its.

GIMME MEAT

GOAT NECK
with Pickled Watermelon
Rind Salad 95

DUCK BREAST
with Brown-Butter Kimchi
and Miso-Marcona Butter. 97

CHAR SIU RIBS
with Apple Slaw. 101

**SLOW-COOKER
PORK SHOULDER** 102

FRIED PORK SHANK
with Kimchi "Wing Sauce" 105

**WHOLE ROASTED
LAMB SHOULDER**. 106

PEANUT PORK RAGOUT 109

**SLOW-ROASTED
BEEF TENDERLOIN**
with Horseradish Crema. 110

CRISPY BEEF SHORT RIBS
with Avocado and
Grapefruit Chermoula. 113

**SLOW-COOKER
COCONUT-BRAISED
BEEF CHEEKS** 116

**YOGURT-MARINATED
CHICKEN THIGHS**
with Cilantro 119

Goats Go MO

———

Grilled Piadina Flatbread 122

Szechuan Sausage Skewers
with Minty Yogurt 125

Kevin's Gumbo 128

Grilled Pork Belly with
Sauce Green, Peaches,
and Blackberries 131

Miso-Butterscotch
Budino with Yogurt and
Blueberry Jam 134

THIS CHAPTER SHOULD REALLY BE CALLED "GIVE GARY MEAT," because in a perfect world, he'd eat only meat. I, on the other hand, am not that interested in going to a restaurant and getting a big plate of rich, fatty meat as the whole story. That's why these dishes have the best of both worlds: big, hearty meats with something nice and refreshing on the side. It's not just about cooking a great piece of meat (though that is totally covered here); it's also about showing how you can balance it with texture and layers of flavor.

What's also important is buying good meat. Is it always possible to get locally farmed meat? No. But shopping at a farmers' market is fun, and when you do you can always freeze a whole bunch of meat for coming months. Or find a great butcher shop in your neighborhood. If you end up buying meat off the shelf at the grocery store, dig to the back and get the freshest ones.

GOAT

1 cup extra-virgin olive oil

½ cup soy sauce

⅓ cup sliced shallots

¼ cup fresh rosemary
leaves

2 tablespoons roughly
chopped garlic

2 tablespoons Dijon
mustard

1 fresh Thai chile

1 whole goat neck
(1½ to 2 pounds)

AIOLI

1 large egg yolk

1 tablespoon Dijon mustard

¼ cup sherry vinegar

1 tablespoon soy sauce

½ tablespoon sambal oelek

½ tablespoon honey

2 cups canola oil

2 sprigs of rosemary, stems
discarded and leaves
finely chopped

Kosher salt

Pickled Watermelon Rind
Salad (recipe follows)

Once a month when it is goat neck day at Girl & the Goat, Gary gets very excited because it's his favorite part of the animal. The meat is really tender and delicious, and it often gets overlooked. It's also ridiculously easy to cook. I marinate the meat overnight, then pop it in the oven wrapped in plastic wrap and foil, which keeps all the moisture in so the meat steams and roasts at the same time and results in succulent, deeply flavored meat. The hardest part is probably finding a goat's neck, but you could absolutely use this recipe with a lamb neck or pork neck instead (ask your butcher). I like to top the goat with pickled watermelon rinds tossed with pepitas for crunch and arugula for its peppery bite. A little bit of the pickling liquid goes into the vinaigrette to pour over the top. *Serves 4 to 6*

GOAT NECK
WITH PICKLED WATERMELON RIND SALAD

Marinate the goat:
Combine the olive oil, soy sauce, shallots, rosemary, garlic, mustard, and chile in a blender and blend until smooth. Transfer the marinade to a large bowl and set the neck in the marinade. Cover with plastic and refrigerate for 12 hours.

Preheat the oven to 300°F.

Remove the neck from the marinade and wrap it in plastic wrap. Ensure that it is fully sealed before wrapping it in a layer of aluminum foil. Put it on a sheet pan and roast for 5 hours, or until the meat is falling off the bone.

Make the aioli:
Combine the egg yolk, mustard, vinegar, soy sauce, sambal oelek, and honey in a blender. Blend on medium speed and then, with the blender still running, slowly drizzle in the oil until the aioli emulsifies. Add the rosemary and season with salt.

Transfer the neck to a serving platter. Drizzle with the aioli, top with the watermelon rind salad, and serve.

Pickled Watermelon Rind Salad

Serves 4 to 6

1 cup Pickled Watermelon Rind (page 262), diced small

¼ cup minced shallots

2 cups torn arugula (rough stems removed)

½ cup toasted and salted pepitas (small shelled pumpkin seeds)

2 tablespoons extra-virgin olive oil

1½ teaspoons fresh lemon juice

Kosher salt

In a medium bowl, toss the pickled rind with the shallots, arugula, pepitas, olive oil, and lemon juice. Season to taste with salt.

2 cups Marcona almonds

3 tablespoons sambal oelek

3 tablespoons white miso paste (see page 98)

3 tablespoons soy sauce

⅓ cup canola oil, or more if needed

5 tablespoons unsalted butter

1 cup kimchi, homemade (page 259) or store-bought

4 skin-on duck breasts

Kosher salt and pepper

I learned how to make a perfectly tender-on-the-inside, crispy-on-the-outside duck breast from my chef friend Dale Levitsky. I had originally been taught to start duck in a cold pan and then cook it low and slow to render all the fat under the skin. Dale said, *No way!* He showed me that if you get the pan so smoking hot that when you put the duck in it makes that crushing *sssshhhh* sound, it'll form a caramelized crust on the skin. Then you put it in the oven—still skin side down—and cook it until it is medium rare on the inside. The skin will be perfectly crisp.

Most people think of eating kimchi cold, but if you toss it quickly in warm browned butter, it makes a simple, balanced pan sauce to go over the duck. Then you take Marcona almonds—which are pricey but worth it because they're full of the oil that makes such a great nut butter—and blend them until they are creamy and smooth in a food processor. That, plus some miso and soy for saltiness and sambal oelek for a little zing, makes for a super-savory, rich, tasty condiment to slather on meats. *Serves 4*

DUCK BREAST

WITH BROWN-BUTTER KIMCHI AND MISO-MARCONA BUTTER

In a food processor, combine the almonds, sambal oelek, miso paste, and soy sauce. Blend until the almonds begin to break down to form a thick, crunchy texture. Add the oil and 3 tablespoons cold water. Continue to process until everything is well incorporated and the texture is similar to that of hummus. If it is too chunky, add a little more oil and another 3 tablespoons cold water.

Cook the butter in a nonstick sauté pan over medium-high heat until dark caramel colored—it should smell nutty, not burnt—3 to 4 minutes. Add the kimchi and toss to coat. Cook for 2 minutes and then remove from the heat.

Preheat the oven to 400°F. Warm a large, ovenproof skillet over medium heat.

(Continues)

While the pan heats, use a sharp knife to score the fat of the duck breasts in a crosshatch pattern, with the cuts about ½ inch apart. Season the duck on both sides with salt and pepper. Put the breasts, fat side down, in the pan to render the fat, about 6 minutes. Turn the duck breasts over and sear for 1 minute. Turn them fat side down again and transfer the pan to the oven to roast until the breasts are medium-rare or a meat thermometer reads 135°F, 7 to 9 minutes. Let the duck breasts rest on a cutting board for 5 minutes before slicing thinly against the grain.

Spread the almond butter on the bottom of a rimmed dish. Lay the sliced duck breast over it and pour the kimchi on top. Serve immediately.

GOOD STUFF: MISO

Pretty much all the time you can find a 22-quart container of miso in the cooler at Girl & the Goat. We buy it in bulk because there's almost nothing that doesn't get just *that* much better with a small spoonful of it. Miso is for so much more than miso soup! You can use it to finish soups and sauces (especially store-bought), take a dessert to a much more interesting place (like the Miso-Butterscotch Budino on page 134), or add it to anything that can use a salty, umami boost. If I'm cooking something that needs a little flavor boost, I always reach for the miso. Who knew soybeans could taste so good?!

There are all different types of miso, but I like white the best because it is mild and slightly sweet. You'll definitely want to buy miso in the Asian section of your store. Look for Japanese brands—not any cheap-o American ones.

½ cup Shaoxing rice wine or dry sherry

½ cup soy sauce

¼ cup dark soy sauce

⅓ cup honey

⅓ cup hoisin sauce

⅓ cup maltose syrup or corn syrup

3 tablespoons red fermented tofu (found in Asian markets or online)

2 tablespoons toasted sesame oil

2 teaspoons Chinese five-spice powder

1 teaspoon ground white pepper

½ tablespoon salt

1 cup canola oil

3 garlic cloves, minced

1 tablespoon minced fresh ginger

2 full slabs baby back ribs or Chinese spareribs (about 3 pounds)

SLAW

2 tablespoons apple cider vinegar

1 tablespoon honey

½ teaspoon kosher salt

4 tart apples, such as Granny Smith, cored and shredded

¼ cup very thinly sliced shallots

1 fennel bulb, very thinly sliced

¼ cup chopped fresh sorrel

2 tablespoons torn fresh mint

This recipe was inspired by the almost neon-red char siu–style roasted pork ribs you get when you go out for Chinese food. They have that perfect mix of spice and tanginess. I cook them the same way as I cook goat's neck—wrapped in plastic and foil—so I can lock in all the flavor and moisture. This is a great make-ahead dish because you can cook the ribs the night before. All you have to do before serving is coat them with the marinade and heat them on a grill or under the broiler to get that signature caramelized exterior.

Serves 4 to 6

CHAR SIU RIBS
WITH APPLE SLAW

Marinate the ribs:
In a blender, combine the wine, both soy sauces, the honey, hoisin sauce, syrup, tofu, sesame oil, five-spice powder, pepper, and salt. Pour half into a small bowl, cover, and refrigerate to use for the glaze. Add the canola oil, garlic, and ginger to the remaining marinade in the blender and blend until smooth. Slather the ribs with the marinade and lay them in a pan. Cover the pan with plastic wrap and refrigerate for 4 hours.

Preheat the oven to 300°F.

Tightly wrap the ribs in plastic wrap and ensure that they are fully sealed. Then wrap the ribs in aluminum foil. Put the ribs on a sheet tray and roast for 4 hours, until fork-tender. Unwrap the ribs and allow them to rest at room temperature for 20 minutes.

Make the slaw:
In a medium bowl, whisk together the vinegar, honey, and salt. Add the apples, shallot, fennel, sorrel, and mint and toss to coat.

Preheat a grill or grill pan to medium heat.

Cut between the ribs to separate them and then brush them with the reserved glaze. Grill until a caramelized crust forms, about 5 minutes, making sure not to burn the sugary glaze. Garnish with the apple slaw and serve.

Gary and I bought a slow cooker at Target for about fifteen bucks, and it was probably one of the best non-investments we've made. We initially got it just to keep something warm for a party, but then one night we had some pork shoulder and thought, *Oh, let's put it in the slow cooker.* I diced the meat, tossed it with a spice mix and a little salt, then threw it in along with some canned tomatoes, onions, and a little bit of blueberry jam I had lying around (because, why not?). The result was a perfectly tender, moist pork shoulder that rendered a flavorful sauce that's delicious over rice or with potatoes. Now the slow cooker is pretty much my best friend, since I can get everything in there while Ernie's sleeping and then spend the rest of the day with him. You know a dish is super-simple if you can make it while tending to an infant! *Serves 4 to 6*

SLOW-COOKER PORK SHOULDER

Season the pork cubes with the spice mix and 2 tablespoons salt. Place into the slow cooker.

In a large bowl, toss the carrots, tomatoes, and onion with 1 tablespoon salt. Add to the slow cooker along with the garlic, jam, tomato paste, wine, chicken stock, and oil. Cook on high for 2½ hours.

Season with salt to taste and add the potatoes. Let the mixture cook for 2½ to 3 hours more, until the potatoes are tender. Serve hot.

3 pounds boneless pork shoulder, cut into 2-inch cubes

1½ tablespoons Razzle Spice Mix (page 43)

Kosher salt

2 cups thinly sliced carrots

1 (14.5-ounce) can diced tomatoes with juices

1 sweet onion, sliced

4 large garlic cloves, thinly sliced

½ cup blueberry jam, homemade (see page 134) or store-bought

1 (6-ounce) can tomato paste

½ cup dry white wine

1 cup chicken stock

2 tablespoons canola oil

3 medium Yukon Gold potatoes, diced large

BRINE

1 teaspoon whole black
   peppercorns

1 teaspoon fennel seeds

1 teaspoon coriander seeds

1 teaspoon crushed red
   pepper flakes

1 Fuji apple, quartered and
   cored

1 small onion, quartered

¼ cup fresh tarragon leaves

2 garlic cloves, smashed

1 (1-inch) piece fresh
   ginger, peeled

⅓ cup kosher salt

2 tablespoons granulated
   sugar

8 cups ice cubes

2 to 4 small pork shanks
   (3 pounds total)

BRAISING LIQUID

8 to 10 cups chicken stock

½ cup roughly chopped
   onion

½ cup roughly chopped
   carrot

½ cup roughly chopped
   fennel bulb

¼ cup dried shiitake
   mushrooms

1 cup coconut milk

2 quarts canola oil, for
   frying

4 tablespoons (½ stick)
   unsalted butter

2 cups Kimchi Sauce
   (page 259)

This has been on the menu at Girl & the Goat almost since it opened, though somewhat different from what I had originally planned. I started by braising the meat as I normally would, but I wanted to see what would happen if I threw the shanks into the deep-fryer afterward. I then put some spices on them, and it tasted like the best fried chicken I never had. (That said, you could definitely skip the frying part; just braise the meat a day before you serve it and reheat it in the oven.) I put these out like a big party platter of wings and let people go to town, picking the meat off the bones and dipping it in a buttery, spicy "wing sauce." *Serves 6 to 8*

FRIED PORK SHANK

WITH KIMCHI "WING SAUCE"

Brine the pork shanks:
In a large pot over medium heat, toast the peppercorns, fennel and coriander seeds, and red pepper flakes until fragrant, about 2 minutes. Add the apple, onion, tarragon, garlic, ginger, salt, sugar, and 4 cups of water to the pot. Cook for 5 minutes over medium heat, or until the salt and sugar dissolve. Remove the pot from the heat and let sit for 15 minutes before adding the ice cubes. Allow the brine to cool completely. Submerge the shanks in the brine and let sit in the brine in the fridge for 12 hours.

Preheat the oven to 275°F.

Braise the pork shanks:
In a large pot or Dutch oven over medium-high heat, combine the stock, onion, carrot, fennel, mushrooms, and coconut milk. Bring to a boil and then lower the heat. Drain the brined shanks and add to the pot. Simmer for 5 minutes. Cover the pot with aluminum foil and then add a tight-fitting lid. Transfer the pot to the oven. Braise the shanks for 3½ hours, until fork tender and nearly falling off the bone. Gently remove the shanks from the braising liquid and let them cool completely.

In a large pot or deep-fryer, heat the oil to 375°F. While the oil heats, melt the butter in a small saucepan over medium-low. Add the sauce and whisk to incorporate. Keep warm over low heat until ready to serve, mixing to reincorporate the butter as needed.

Carefully drop the pork shanks in the hot oil and fry until golden brown and crispy, about 5 minutes. Serve with the sauce.

I always found myself skipping lamb shoulder as an option for dinner parties or large family dinners because a giant hunk of meat can be intimidating—you never know if it's going to come out tasty. But then I learned the secret to making a great piece of lamb, especially a great big hunky one like shoulder, which has so much more flavor than the usual cuts like chops. The trick is to enhance the richness of the meat, rather than trying to cover it up. I do that by brining the meat first, which infuses it with lots of savory notes (like fish sauce), and helps it taste oh-so-*meaty*. Then, as an homage to my mom and the lamb chops she always served with mint jelly, I pair this dish with mint chimichurri. It's the perfect mix of fresh herbs, garlic, and red pepper flakes and it brightens everything up. *Serves 6*

WHOLE ROASTED LAMB SHOULDER

Brine the lamb:

In a large pot over medium-high heat, combine the marmalade, salt, sugar, garlic, fish sauce, mustard, and sambal oelek with 8 cups water. Bring to a boil and whisk until the sugar and salt dissolve, about 5 minutes. Remove the pot from the heat and let the brine cool for 15 minutes. Add the mint and ice cubes to the pot. Allow the brine to cool fully, then submerge the lamb in the brine. Let the lamb brine in the refrigerator for a full 24 hours.

Preheat the oven to 425°F.

Remove the lamb from the brine and transfer it to a roasting rack set inside a large roasting pan. Roast the lamb, uncovered, for 1 hour.

Fill the bottom of the pan with enough water to come up about 2 inches in the pan (but not enough to submerge the lamb). Carefully tent the pan in foil. Reduce the oven temperature to 275°F and roast for another 5 hours. The lamb should be fork-tender and shred easily when pried with a fork.

Make the chimichurri:

In a medium bowl, combine the mint, parsley, oregano, shallot, preserved lemon, and garlic. Add the olive oil, lime juice, vinegar, honey, fish sauce, and red pepper flakes and mix until incorporated. Season with salt to taste. Serve with the lamb.

LAMB

1½ cups orange marmalade

1½ cups kosher salt

1 cup sugar

1 cup garlic cloves, peeled (about 2 heads of garlic)

1 cup fish sauce

¼ cup Dijon mustard

2 tablespoons sambal oelek

1 cup torn fresh mint leaves

8 cups ice cubes

5- to 7-pound bone-in lamb shoulder or leg

CHIMICHURRI

2 cups finely chopped fresh mint

¼ cup finely chopped fresh parsley

2 tablespoons minced fresh oregano

¼ cup minced shallots

1 tablespoon minced preserved lemon, homemade (page 198) or store-bought

1 large garlic clove, minced

¾ cup extra-virgin olive oil

3 tablespoons fresh lime juice

2 tablespoons red wine vinegar

1 tablespoon honey

½ tablespoon fish sauce

½ teaspoon crushed red pepper flakes

Kosher salt

GOOD STUFF: FISH SAUCE

Anyone who's ever been around when we get food deliveries at the restaurants has probably seen the enormous pallets of fish sauce. It's just about my favorite ingredient, so it shows up on all three of my menus. Fish sauce is an awesome way to add funky, salty flavor even to non-Asian dishes. I love it so much that I thought about packaging this book with a bottle of fish sauce, just so everyone would have some when they got home. Come to think of it, that'd make a pretty great gift.

Just like wines or olive oils, all fish sauces taste different. I think Red Boat is by far the best one on the market, especially the 41N, which is a little bit lighter than their original blend and still contains no added sugar, unlike other products.

1 pound ground pork

1½ tablespoons minced garlic

1 tablespoon minced shallot

1 cup chicken stock

½ cup halved cherry tomatoes

¼ cup roasted peanuts, chopped

¼ cup tamarind pulp, or 2 tablespoons tamarind paste

2 tablespoons white miso

1½ tablespoons harissa, homemade (page 58) or store-bought

1 tablespoon tomato paste

1½ tablespoons sugar

1½ tablespoons fresh lime juice

Kosher salt

This is definitely a standout on the Girl & the Goat menu. It's sweet and sour, and the peanuts contrast really nicely with the pork flavor-wise, in addition to giving it great crunchy texture. Heap this over noodles, some roasted squash or a sweet potato, or eat it like a stew with a little fresh slaw on top. *Serves 4*

PEANUT PORK RAGOUT

In a dry medium saucepan over medium-high heat, cook the pork, stirring occasionally, until browned, 6 to 8 minutes. Do not drain the fat. Add the garlic and shallot and cook until soft, about 2 minutes. Stir in the stock, cherry tomatoes, peanuts, tamarind, miso, harissa, tomato paste, and sugar. Add the lime juice and season with salt to taste.

Reduce the heat to low and cook, uncovered, for 20 to 30 minutes. The sauce should thicken significantly. Adjust the seasoning if necessary, and serve.

Beef tenderloin—while delicious—is an investment, so whenever I cook it, I want to make sure that I don't mess it up! Your best bet for doing justice to this cut at home is to cook it low and slow. It's foolproof and all but guarantees that it'll be juicy and tender. I also love marinating the meat with horseradish—a classic combo with beef—and fermented black beans (one of my favorite salty ingredients; see page 61) and letting it sit overnight. It pre-seasons the meat perfectly. *Serves 4*

SLOW-ROASTED BEEF TENDERLOIN
WITH HORSERADISH CREMA

Marinate the beef:

Drain the beans and discard the water. Combine the beans, soy sauce, horseradish, vinegar, and both oils in a blender and blend until smooth. Transfer the marinade to a large bowl or container, add the tenderloin, and turn to coat. Let the meat marinate in the fridge for at least 30 minutes.

Preheat the oven to 250°F.

Remove the meat from the marinade and put it in a roasting pan. Roast for 2 hours, or until a thermometer reads 120 to 125°F. Allow the tenderloin to rest for 15 minutes before slicing.

Make the horseradish crema:

In a medium bowl, whisk together the sour cream, horseradish, cream, and lemon juice. Season to taste with salt and pepper.

Serve the crema on the side of the tenderloin as a dip.

BEEF

2 tablespoons fermented black beans, soaked in hot water for 30 minutes

⅓ cup soy sauce

¼ cup prepared horseradish

¼ cup sherry vinegar

¼ cup canola oil

2 tablespoons toasted sesame oil

2- to 3-pound whole beef tenderloin, trimmed of silver skin and fat by the butcher

HORSERADISH CREMA

2 cups sour cream

¼ cup prepared horseradish

¼ cup heavy cream

2 tablespoons fresh lemon juice

Kosher salt and pepper

TIP

When you ask your butcher for the beef tenderloin, make sure he or she saves the "chain" that usually gets trimmed off. Buy it and cube it to make beef skewers.

SHORT RIBS

4 tablespoons canola oil

2 pounds boneless beef
short ribs

2 tablespoons salt

1 tablespoon pepper

1 fennel bulb, quartered

1 yellow onion, quartered

2 carrots, roughly chopped

4 quarts beef stock

1 cup dry red wine

½ cup tomato paste

SPICE MIX

½ cinnamon stick

2 dried chiles de árbol

1 teaspoon chopped dried
orange peel

1 teaspoon mustard seeds

¼ teaspoon black
peppercorns

1 tablespoon ground sumac

1 teaspoon tomato powder

1 teaspoon smoked paprika

2 quarts canola oil, for
frying

Kosher salt

Onion and Herb-Marinated
Avocados (recipe
follows)

Grapefruit Chermoula
(recipe follows)

This dish is more like a salad than a meat dish, but that doesn't mean meat takes a backseat. It's just a lighter take on short ribs. First, you dice braised short ribs and toss them in the deep-fryer until they're crispy. Then you coat them in a spice mix that gives some heat along with nice, warm baking spice notes, so the meaty bits become almost like beef croutons. They are then put over a light, refreshing mix of onion and herb-marinated avocados and topped with a grapefruit sauce that brings just the right amount of acid. It's a play on a chermoula I had in Belize that was a lot lighter and brighter than the Moroccan kind I knew, with tons of lime juice, cilantro, and shallots. *Serves 4*

CRISPY BEEF SHORT RIBS

WITH AVOCADO AND GRAPEFRUIT CHERMOULA

Preheat the oven to 325°F.

Braise the short ribs:
Heat 2 tablespoons of the oil in a large sauté pan over high heat. Season both sides of the ribs with the salt and pepper. Working in batches, brown the short ribs, about 5 minutes per side. Transfer the browned short ribs to a roasting pan.

In the same sauté pan, over medium heat, cook the fennel, onion, and carrots in the rib drippings until just tender, about 5 minutes. Transfer the veggies to the roasting pan with the ribs.

Put the roasting pan over medium-high heat and add the stock, wine, and tomato paste. Bring the mixture to a boil, then remove the pan from the heat. Cover with a tight-fitting lid or aluminum foil and transfer the pan to the oven. Roast the short ribs in the oven for 3½ hours. The meat should be fork-tender but not completely falling apart. If the meat isn't finished, cook in 30-minute increments until done. Remove the ribs from the braising liquid and let them cool completely.

(Continues)

Make the spice mix:

In a spice grinder or food processor, grind the cinnamon stick, chiles, orange peel, mustard seeds, and peppercorns until they're a fairly uniform powder.

Mix with the sumac, tomato powder, and paprika.

For the short ribs:

In a large pot, heat the canola oil to 350°F.

Cut the meat into 1-inch cubes and, working in batches if necessary so you don't crowd the pot, fry until crispy, about 4 minutes. Immediately strain the cubes and toss them with the spice mix. Season with salt, if desired.

Spread the avocados over the bottom of a platter. Sprinkle the crispy short ribs over the top and drizzle with the chermoula. Serve immediately.

Onion and Herb-Marinated Avocados

Serves 4

2 ripe Hass avocados

1 ruby red grapefruit

2 tablespoons fresh lemon juice

½ teaspoon kosher salt

½ cup shaved red onion

2 tablespoons roughly chopped fresh mint leaves

2 tablespoons roughly chopped fresh cilantro leaves

Halve the avocados lengthwise, remove the pits, and discard. Using the tip of your knife, make three diagonal slices through each side of the avocado, then three more in a crosshatch pattern. Invert and gently remove the cubes from the skin with a spoon.

To supreme citrus: Using a knife, thinly cut off the top and bottom of the grapefruit to create two flat surfaces that expose the flesh inside. Following the curve of the fruit, run your knife between the skin and the flesh until the grapefruit is completely peeled. Hold the grapefruit in your hand and carefully slice between the white membrane to create segments.

In a medium bowl, toss the avocado cubes with the lemon juice and salt. Mix in the onion, mint, cilantro, and grapefruit sections.

Grapefruit Chermoula

Makes 1½ cups

1 cup fresh grapefruit juice

¼ cup fresh lime juice

3 tablespoons minced shallots

½ teaspoon minced garlic

3 tablespoons chopped fresh
mint leaves

1½ tablespoons roughly
chopped fresh cilantro

1 teaspoon roughly chopped
pickled jalapeño, homemade
(page 264) or store-bought

¼ teaspoon kosher salt

In a medium bowl, combine the juices, shallot, garlic, mint,
cilantro, jalapeño, and salt.

This is like a more flavorful, more Asian version of beef Stroganoff, which I love making with beef cheeks, a tough (and cheap) cut of meat that gets nice and tender when you cook it gently over time. Using coconut cream as the main braising liquid is a great way to add richness to a dish and make a super-rich, slightly sweet, beefy gravy. You could serve these with a side of rice and some Fresh Flour Tortillas (page 173), and let people make their own little taco snacks, or you could do what Gary does and buy those extra-large tortillas and make Ernie-size burritos. *Serves 4 to 6*

SLOW-COOKER COCONUT-BRAISED BEEF CHEEKS

Heat the oil in a large sauté pan over high heat. Season the cheeks with salt and pepper and, working in batches so you don't crowd the pan, brown the cheeks for 4 minutes on each side. Remove the cheeks from the pan.

Combine the browned cheeks with the remaining ingredients in a slow cooker. Set on high and cook until very tender, about 5 hours.

2 tablespoons canola oil

4 pounds beef cheeks, silver skin removed, or boneless short ribs

Kosher salt and pepper

3 (12-ounce) cans cream of coconut

½ cup fish sauce

1 tablespoon minced garlic

1 tablespoon sambal oelek

2 teaspoons minced fresh ginger

TIP

The leftover cooking liquid is like a beef-infused coconut broth, some of which you can serve over the cheeks, then use the extra to make a soup or spoon over rice or pasta.

- 2 packed cups roughly chopped fresh cilantro (about 1 bunch)
- 1½ cups plain Greek yogurt
- ⅓ cup finely grated Parmesan cheese
- ⅓ cup extra-virgin olive oil
- ¼ cup fish sauce
- 1 shallot, sliced
- 4 garlic cloves, peeled
- 2 tablespoons sambal oelek
- Grated zest of 1 lemon
- 1½ pounds skin-on boneless chicken thighs
- 2 tablespoons canola oil

Gary is obsessed with chicken thighs. We pretty much always have a package of them in the fridge. In fact, while I was writing this, he came by and said, "Don't forget we have those chicken thighs in the fridge." I'm not exaggerating! One of our favorite ways to prepare them is to marinate them in yogurt with cilantro and fish sauce. The yogurt helps give great flavor while also tenderizing the meat, and the fish sauce seeps into the chicken so you don't need to season it before it gets cooked. I highly recommend buying boneless thighs with the skin still on, because the skin gives the meat great flavor and juiciness, yet the thighs cook in no time.

Serves 2

YOGURT-MARINATED CHICKEN THIGHS
WITH CILANTRO

In a blender, puree the cilantro, yogurt, Parmesan, olive oil, fish sauce, shallot, garlic, sambal oelek, and lemon zest until smooth.

Pour into a large bowl, add the chicken thighs, and toss to coat. Let marinate overnight, covered, in the fridge.

Preheat the oven to 375°F.

Heat the canola oil in a large nonstick skillet over medium-high heat. Without removing any of the marinade from the thighs, brown them for 2 to 3 minutes per side. Do this in batches to avoid crowding the pan. When all the chicken has been browned, transfer it to a large baking dish and bake until cooked through, 8 minutes.

Serve the thighs whole or sliced.

GOATS GO MO

. . . .

When Gary got the call from Phil Wymore, the brewmaster at Perennial Artisan Ales in St. Louis, asking if he wanted to come down to Missouri for the weekend and make some beer, he obviously couldn't say no. So, we decided to make a family trip of it—and get in a really good meal, too. I reached out to my friend Kevin Willmann, the chef-owner of Farmhaus, who always seems to be game for a good time. Kevin and I were named *Food & Wine*'s Best New Chef in the same year, and we've been tight ever since. Every time we get together, it involves a lot of eating and drinking; and I love cooking in his kitchen because it's super laid-back—all T-shirts and Busch beer, and making tasty food with whatever his farmers are bringing by. (Plus, Gary gets to play with all of Kevin's power tools while we work.) For this trip, Kevin and I decided to get all our food people together with Gary and Phil's beer people for a little backyard hangout. Brewers like food, and chefs definitely like beer—so it works. Then we put together a menu that was fun and casual—the kind of food people can just grab as it's ready and eat standing up. Phil brought some seasonal beers he wanted to show off, and by the time the rainstorm passed us by, everyone was full, happy—and a little tipsy.

Meats + sauce + flatbread = never a bad thing, so I often make this simple Italian flatbread for parties. It's fun to be rolling out and cooking these when friends come over—they can even join in on the fun! *Makes 14 to 16 flatbreads*

2 cups all-purpose flour, plus more for kneading

2½ teaspoons baking powder

½ teaspoon kosher salt

3 tablespoons extra-virgin olive oil

GRILLED PIADINA FLATBREAD

Put the flour in a medium bowl. Using your hands, mix in the baking powder and salt. Dig a small well in the center and stream in the olive oil and ¾ cup water, mixing with your free hand to make a smooth dough. Cover in plastic wrap and let rest at room temperature for 20 minutes.

Transfer the dough to a lightly floured work surface and gently knead for 2 minutes. Return the dough to the bowl and cover. Let the dough rest at room temperature for another 20 minutes, knead again, and return the dough to the bowl for 20 more minutes.

Preheat a grill or grill pan to medium heat.

Put the dough on the floured surface and break it into golf ball–size portions. Lay the balls on a sheet tray and cover with plastic wrap for 15 minutes.

Using a rolling pin, roll the dough balls into ½-inch-thick rounds.

Grill the dough until the flatbread is firm but still pillowy, about 3 minutes per side. Serve warm.

- 1¼ pounds 80% lean ground goat or pork
- 1 tablespoon minced shallot
- ½ tablespoon minced garlic
- ½ tablespoon grated fresh ginger
- ¾ teaspoon kosher salt
- ¾ teaspoon crushed red pepper flakes, preferably Korean, or to taste
- ¾ teaspoon ground Szechuan peppercorns
- 3 tablespoons Shaoxing rice wine or dry sherry
- Canola oil (optional)
- Minty Yogurt (recipe follows)
- Szechuan Chile Sauce (recipe follows)
- Fresh mint, to garnish

Before opening Duck Duck Goat, Gary and I headed to China with some fellow goats for two weeks in search of inspiration. The highlight for us was the Szechuan province, known for its crazy bold flavors, where we ate just about every noodle and dumpling that crossed our path. I particularly love Szechuan peppercorns, which are like fun little spice bombs—but instead of packing a ton of heat, they make your mouth go all tingly and numb. That's what inspired this spicy sausage blend, which we usually make with goat meat, but it's just as good with pork. Yes, you can buy a spicy Italian sausage from the store, but I strongly urge you to consider making your own instead. It's super-easy to do (not scary) and you can use the leftovers to make a round of "This Little Piggy Went to China" breakfast sandwiches (Szechuan-Style Breakfast Biscuits, page 13). *Makes 24 skewers*

SZECHUAN SAUSAGE SKEWERS
WITH MINTY YOGURT

In a food processor, combine the meat, shallot, garlic, ginger, salt, red pepper flakes, and peppercorns. Pulse until well combined. Turn the machine on and drizzle in 1 tablespoon of ice water and the rice wine until well mixed and the meat is emulsified. Transfer to the fridge to chill for at least 1 hour and up to 2 days before cooking.

Soak 24 bamboo skewers in cold water for 1 hour to help prevent scorching.

Scoop the cold sausage into 24 portions. Form each into a 2-inch-long cylinder around the tip of a drained bamboo skewer. Return to the fridge for at least 1 hour before cooking. The sausage will hold its shape and grill up better if chilled.

Heat a grill to medium-high heat.

Arrange the sausage skewers around the outside of the grill, so the sticks are over the edge and do not burn. (If the grill grates are hot enough, the cooked meat will release cleanly without the need for oil; otherwise, lightly brush the grates with canola

(Continues)

oil before placing the skewers on them.) Allow the meat to cook thoroughly before you attempt to move it; otherwise it will stick. Sear the first side for at least 6 minutes, then turn and cook again for 6 to 7 more minutes, until both sides have a dark crust.

To serve, schmear a thick strip of mint yogurt sauce down one side of a platter. Put the meat end of each skewer in the yogurt. Drizzle with the chile sauce, and garnish with the mint. Serve hot.

Minty Yogurt

Makes 2 cups

2 cups plain full-fat Greek yogurt	¼ cup finely chopped fresh mint leaves
1 tablespoon fresh lemon juice	Kosher salt

Whisk together all the ingredients and store covered in the fridge for up to 3 days.

Szechuan Chile Sauce

Every morning we were in Chengdu, we'd go to this little place next to the hotel for breakfast. And every morning, we'd have pork dumplings that had nothing but chile sauce on them. It was the simplest thing ever, but so good. This is my take on that amazing sauce, a mix of chile oil, malt vinegar, fish sauce, sesame oil, and Szechuan peppercorns; it has a savory, just-right-amount-of-spicy quality that's really addicting. Okay, so they don't use fish sauce in China, but I think everything tastes better with fish sauce!

This sauce shows up three times in this book—straight up with these skewers, slightly sweetened with maple syrup for a breakfast sandwich (see page 13), and with a cool twist of blueberry jam for grilled salmon (see page 149). All the more reason to make a batch to keep in your fridge and use it on anything and everything. *Makes 2 cups*

⅓ cup broad bean paste, found in Asian markets or online

⅓ cup fish sauce

¾ cup malt vinegar

¼ cup toasted sesame oil

¼ cup chile oil

3 cups chopped fresh flat-leaf parsley

2 tablespoons toasted sesame seeds

1 tablespoon ground Szechuan peppercorns

Whisk together all the ingredients. The sauce will keep, covered in the fridge, for up to 1 week.

Kevin's food is just as informed by his farming-family roots as it is by the backwaters, bayous, and bays that he fell in love with after moving to Pensacola, Florida. When we met, we instantly connected over our approach to food, especially taking a new look at traditional preparations, which sums up this gumbo to a T. Kevin likes to build the flavor first with the "holy trinity" (celery, red peppers, and onions) and then thicken with the roux later. He also uses McCormick's gumbo filé (as Kevin says, "Don't f'ing bother making it yourself") and insists you put parsley on it because "that's just how it is." Serving the gumbo over rice and garnished with herbs is the ideal way to enjoy it. *Serves 4 to 6*

KEVIN'S GUMBO

In a small sauté pan over low heat, melt the butter. Whisk in the flour and cook, whisking, until the mixture smells nutty and has an almond color, about 15 minutes.

In a large pot over medium-high heat, heat 4 tablespoons of the olive oil. Add the onions and sauté until they begin to brown, about 10 minutes. Add the bell peppers and continue sautéing until they brown slightly, 6 minutes. Add the remaining 2 tablespoons oil, the garlic, and 1 tablespoon salt. Stir constantly for 2 to 3 more minutes to lightly brown the garlic, making sure the garlic does not burn or stick to the pan.

Deglaze the pot with the wine, scraping all the browned bits from the bottom with a wooden spoon. Add more wine or a little water if the liquid evaporates too quickly. Add the stock, fish trimmings, paprika, and black pepper and bring to a simmer, stirring often, being careful not to break up the fish too much. Gently stir in the filé and add the celery and okra. Simmer for 5 more minutes, then add the Worcestershire. Season with salt.

Ladle off about a quart of liquid—as free from fish and vegetables as possible—into a small saucepan over medium heat. Bring to a simmer and then whisk 2 tablespoons of the butter-flour mixture into the liquid until it is thick enough to coat a spoon.

Reincorporate the thickened liquid in the large pot and cook for 3 more minutes as the whole batch thickens. You may need to add some of the remaining roux if the gumbo is still too thin. The rest of the roux can be frozen for up to 2 months.

4 tablespoons (½ stick) unsalted butter

¼ cup all-purpose flour

6 tablespoons olive oil

2 medium white onions, diced

2 medium red bell peppers, chopped

3 tablespoons minced garlic

Kosher salt

¼ cup dry white wine, or more if needed

2 quarts fish or chicken stock

6 pounds fish fillet, such as grouper, snapper, tuna, wahoo, flounder, or pompano, cut into ½-inch-thick pieces

2 tablespoons sweet Hungarian paprika

1 teaspoon freshly ground black pepper

1 tablespoon plus 1 teaspoon McCormick's gumbo filé

4 celery stalks, chopped

1 pound fresh okra, sliced

½ cup Worcestershire sauce

Chopped fresh parsley, for garnish

GOOD STUFF: FISH STOCK

I love this dish because it puts leftovers to great use. Any time there are scraps from butchering fish at the restaurant or any little nubbins that don't make a portion, Kevin adds them to a big bag in the freezer (just as we do with the Hamachi Collar, page 150). Then every six months or so, he cooks them into an intensely flavored fish stock, or fumet (pronounced FOO-may). It becomes the perfect fishy base for so many dishes, like this gumbo.

1½ pounds boneless pork belly, thinly sliced

Kalbi Marinade (page 71)

2 small heads radicchio, halved from the core to the end

2 small firm peaches, halved and pitted

Canola oil

Sauce Green (recipe follows)

1 pint blackberries, halved

¼ cup fresh basil leaves, torn

INTERESTING STUFF: COOKING WITH FRUIT

I once worked as a private chef for a woman whose first instruction to me was "no fruit in our savory food." It was a huge bummer, because I love fruit in savory dishes—in salads, over grilled steak, mixed into sauce; it gives you layers of flavor without being overpoweringly sweet. For this grilled pork belly dish, the fruit helps balance the fatty meat and salty, herbaceous sauce, lending just the right amount of acidity and sweetness to round things out. When I saw peaches and blackberries in Kevin's kitchen, I reached for those, but strawberries would also be really good if they're in season, as would blueberries.

When most people think of pork belly, they think of braising it for hours, or curing it, smoking it, and making it into bacon. It makes sense—such a fatty cut needs some love to be tender and delicious. But little do they know; you can also just throw that belly straight onto the grill. The high heat softens the fat enough that you can bite through it, but not so much that there's none left to melt in your mouth. I also give it a slick of marinade originally created for kalbi—Korean barbecued beef short ribs—a minute or two before cooking, which caramelizes with just the right amount of sweetness. Put it over a good schmear of herbed poblano sauce (a.k.a. Sauce Green) and pile it into a taco, heap it onto a bun, or just eat it with your fingers. Whatever you do, save some leftovers to toss with eggs the next morning. *Serves 6 to 8*

GRILLED PORK BELLY
WITH SAUCE GREEN, PEACHES, AND BLACKBERRIES

Heat a grill to medium-high heat.

Soak the pork belly in the marinade for 5 minutes.

Lightly brush the radicchio and peaches with oil and grill just until grill marks form, about 5 minutes. Flip and repeat on the other side. Remove from the grill and let cool.

Grill the marinated pork belly for 2 to 3 minutes per side, making sure the fat begins to render and caramelize.

Slice the radicchio into medium square pieces, the peaches into thick slices, and the pork belly into 2-inch-long pieces. Toss them together.

Schmear the green sauce over the bottom of a large platter. Plate the grilled items over the sauce and top with the blackberries and basil.

Sauce Green

There was already a salsa verde at Girl & the Goat when I invented this also-green sauce, so to avoid confusion—and as a play on salsa verde's English translation—we call it Sauce Green. It's intensely salty, herby, and tasty; a little goes a long way. Try it with simple grilled kebabs, as an updated substitute for mint jelly with lamb, or as a dip with chips. Just make sure all your ingredients are cold when you process them together, otherwise you'll end up with Sauce Brown. *Makes 1 cup*

1 small poblano chile

⅓ cup extra-virgin olive oil, plus a little more

½ bunch flat-leaf parsley, with stems

Pinch of salt

1 tablespoon fish sauce

1 tablespoon malt vinegar

1 teaspoon sambal oelek

1 teaspoon finely chopped fresh rosemary

⅓ cup fresh tarragon leaves

Coat the poblano with a little oil and, under a hot broiler or over a flame on your stove, blister the pepper until the skin begins to peel away and the flesh softens. When well roasted, put the pepper in a bowl and cover with plastic wrap. Allow it to come to room temperature, then carefully peel off the skin and remove the core and seeds. Refrigerate the pepper until you're ready to blend the rest of the sauce.

Heat the ⅓ cup olive oil over medium-high heat in a small sauté pan. Add the parsley, season with a pinch of salt, and cook only until wilted. Use a fine-mesh strainer to strain the parsley from the oil and reserve both. Put them in the fridge until fully cooled.

Roughly chop the parsley. Add the chopped parsley to the blender along with the poblano, fish sauce, vinegar, and sambal oelek, and blend until very smooth. Add the rosemary, tarragon, and flavored oil and blend for a few more seconds. The sauce holds for up to 2 days in the refrigerator.

When Matthew Rice, my former pastry chef, first started working at Girl & the Goat, I told him about how much I love using Asian ingredients in unexpected ways. This pudding was the first thing he came up with, and it became an instant classic. It's got just enough miso to make it taste like butterscotch (and not a bowl of soup), with an alluring, slightly salty, hard-to-put-your-finger-on flavor. I recommend making this and pouring it into individual jars or ramekins to set ahead of time, so they're ready to pass around once the party's started. Play around with the fruit or jam you put on top—just about anything in season will work. *Serves 8*

MISO-BUTTERSCOTCH BUDINO
WITH YOGURT AND BLUEBERRY JAM

Make the budino:
Soak the gelatin in 2 tablespoons water for 10 minutes, until dissolved.

Combine the cream and brown sugar in a medium saucepan and bring to a simmer. Whisk in the butter, miso, vanilla, and salt. Allow to come just about back to a simmer, then remove from the heat.

Strain the mixture through a fine-mesh strainer into a medium bowl. While still warm, stir in the gelatin.

Fill a large bowl halfway with ice cubes and water and set the bowl with the custard mixture in it. Let the custard chill until cool to the touch, then ladle it into serving dishes. Transfer the dishes to the fridge to chill until set, at least 2 hours or overnight.

Make the blueberry jam:
Combine the jam ingredients in a small saucepan and stir in 1 teaspoon water. Cook over medium heat until the fruit has burst and is saucy, about 10 minutes.

Make the honey yogurt:
Whisk together the yogurt and honey, and allow to sit for 5 minutes. Whisk again to fully incorporate.

To serve, top each budino with a dollop of honey yogurt and a drizzle of blueberry jam.

BUDINO

4 teaspoons unflavored gelatin powder

3¼ cups heavy cream

1 cup dark brown sugar

8 tablespoons (1 stick) unsalted butter, cut into pieces

1½ tablespoons white miso paste

1 teaspoon vanilla extract

¼ teaspoon kosher salt

Ice cubes

BLUEBERRY JAM

½ cup fresh blueberries

2 tablespoons granulated sugar

1 teaspoon fresh lemon juice

Pinch of salt

HONEY YOGURT

1 cup plain full-fat Greek yogurt

2 teaspoons powdered honey

GOOD STUFF: POWDERED HONEY

When I first opened Girl & the Goat, I created all the desserts myself (shudder). I remember we were doing some doughnuts with caramelized figs, and I wanted to make the yogurt topping a little bit sweeter. But I didn't like how honey and granulated sugar made it all goopy. I was shopping at an Asian market when I saw honey powder, and I figured I'd try it. Major success. It has all the concentrated honey goodness flavor without the extra goop. Plus, if you eat it right after sprinkling it over something, you get some really nice crunch. Buy a bag and you'll be tempted to put it on just about anything—cereal, oatmeal, ice cream—if you haven't eaten it right out of the bag first.

EATING WITH THE FISHES

I GREW UP EATING A TON OF FISH BECAUSE MY MOM REALLY LOVED it. We always joked that she was going to open a restaurant called Susan's Snappers. It made a lot of sense: We lived on the East Coast, where fresh seafood has a place on almost every menu, and she knew that if you start with really great ingredients, then you don't have to do much to make them taste great. I've definitely inherited my mom's love of all things seafood and have stuffed my menus to the gills with soft-shell crab, lobster, oysters, clams, and mussels. And at home, one of our favorite meals was hanging out in front of the TV with a big ol' pile of crab legs and mounds of butter.

What's that you say? You don't like fish? Maybe you just haven't found the kind you like yet. Fish can be light and flaky or rich and oily. Some is great with the skin on, some with the skin off. Some fish is best grilled, other fish is better steamed in a flavorful broth. And then there's the major component of the *quality* of your fish. The easiest way to figure out what's going to be good is finding fishmongers who know their stuff. They will not only be able to help you figure out what to buy but also what you could substitute if, say, a recipe calls for bass but there's none off the boats that day.

3 blood oranges, segmented (see page 114), juice reserved

½ cup fresh lime juice

¼ cup minced shallots

1 tablespoon minced jalapeño

1 pound dry-packed sea scallops, preferably diver scallops

2 tablespoons roughly chopped fresh cilantro

2 tablespoons thinly sliced scallions (white and green parts)

Kosher salt

Scallops are great for ceviche, or a method of "cooking" your seafood in acid. I like how they have a firmness but also a little sweetness. We use blood orange to balance the acidity of the lime juice; it also helps you feel like you're sitting in the sunshine while eating a winter dish. You can serve this ceviche as is, or better yet, with a side of Masa Chips for scooping (page 167). *Serves 4 as an appetizer*

SCALLOP CEVICHE
WITH BLOOD ORANGE

In a medium bowl, toss together the orange segments, lime juice, shallots, and jalapeño.

Slice the scallops crosswise through the center. Cut each half into quarters. Add the scallops to the orange mixture and let them sit for 30 minutes. Add the cilantro and scallion, season with salt, and serve.

I first made this when I was catering a southern-style wedding, essentially swapping out the traditional Old Bay Seasoning for Creole spice in a chilled crab salad. I tossed in the "holy trinity" of (pickled red) onions, celery, and sweet bell peppers with the spice mix (which I've included here, but you could always buy), and added just enough mayo to coat everything but not make a heavy dressing. What really makes this salad pop, though, is some pickled jalapeños. Serve this with buttery crackers, over some diced avocado, on top of a bed of greens, or heaped onto a buttered roll. *Serves 4*

2 tablespoons Creole Spice Mix (recipe follows)

½ cup mayonnaise

½ cup thinly sliced peeled celery

¼ cup thinly sliced red bell pepper

½ cup Pickled Red Onions (page 258), roughly chopped

2 tablespoons minced Pickled Jalapeños (page 264)

Kosher salt

24 ounces picked-through lump crabmeat

CREOLE CRAB SALAD

In a large bowl, whisk the spice mix into the mayo. Fold in the celery, bell pepper, red onions, and jalapeños. Season with salt, fold in the crabmeat, and serve.

Creole Spice Mix

Makes about ⅔ cup

3 tablespoons smoked paprika

2 tablespoons seasoned salt

1 tablespoon granulated garlic

1 tablespoon granulated onion

1 tablespoon tomato powder

1 tablespoon ground oregano

½ tablespoon dried thyme, ground

½ tablespoon cayenne pepper

½ tablespoon black pepper

In a small bowl, mix all the ingredients. Store in a lidded jar in a cool, dry place.

SHRIMP

1 pound jumbo shrimp
(21–25 count), peeled
and deveined

2 large egg whites

2 tablespoons sambal oelek

1½ tablespoons Shaoxing
rice wine or dry sherry

1½ tablespoons soy sauce

1½ tablespoons fish sauce

1½ tablespoons heavy
cream

1 tablespoon chopped
preserved lemon zest,
homemade (see page
198) or store-bought

1 teaspoon toasted sesame
oil

½ teaspoon sugar

Kosher salt

2 teaspoons canola oil

AIOLI

1 cup good-quality
mayonnaise

1½ teaspoons fish sauce

1 teaspoon sambal oelek

½ teaspoon toasted sesame
oil

8 slices good-quality white
bread

8 tablespoons (1 stick)
unsalted butter

3 tablespoons roughly
chopped fresh cilantro

3 tablespoons roughly
chopped scallion greens

Shrimp toast—which you can find on the menu at many Chinese restaurants—is basically ground-up shrimp on bread that's been deep-fried in oil. I make ours at Duck Duck Goat a bit fancier, mixing a shrimp mousse with some soy sauce, a little chile and cream, and some egg white to fluff it up. Then I schmear it on a piece of white bread, pan-fry the toast in butter until the mousse puffs up a bit, then flip it. After that comes a drizzle of fish sauce aioli and some chopped red bell pepper and pickled veggies. If you're feeling crazy, make two pieces of shrimp toast, throw some mayo and tomato in the middle, and have a kick-ass shrimp sandwich. *Serves 4*

SHRIMP TOAST

Make the shrimp mousse:
Slice a third of the shrimp into ¼-inch-thick pieces and set aside on ice or return to the fridge.

In a food processor, combine the remaining shrimp, the egg whites, sambal oelek, rice wine, soy sauce, fish sauce, cream, lemon zest, sesame oil, sugar, and ½ teaspoon salt. Process until smooth. Transfer to a bowl and fold in the reserved sliced shrimp.

Heat the canola oil in a small sauté pan over medium-high heat. Add a small dollop of the mousse and cook through, about 2 minutes. Taste and add more salt to the entire batch, if necessary.

Make the aioli:
In a small bowl, whisk together the mayonnaise, fish sauce, sambal oelek, and sesame oil.

Spread the shrimp mousse on each slice of bread in a ½-inch-thick layer.

Heat a large griddle or nonstick sauté pan over medium-high heat and add about a third of the butter. When the butter melts and starts to sizzle, put 2 or 3 pieces of the bread, mousse side down, in the pan. Cook until the mousse puffs, 5 to 6 minutes, before flipping and browning the toast side to a golden color, 3 to 4 minutes. Once fully cooked, the shrimp mousse will be firm and reddish in color. Repeat until each piece of toast is cooked.

Slice each toast into 3 strips. Drizzle with the aioli and garnish with the cilantro and scallions. Serve hot.

The entire staff at Girl & the Goat can't wait for these to come on the menu every spring—I know I get excited! Crab Rangoon is one of my favorite things to order at a Chinese restaurant, and since people usually stuff squash blossoms with soft cheeses like ricotta, I figured why not make a crab–cream cheese filling? I add slivered almonds for some texture and serve the whole thing over chive yogurt with a drizzle of soy-lemon vinaigrette for a little acidity and freshness to offset the fried-cheesy richness. If you can't get squash blossoms, you could still make the filling and use it in all sorts of other ways, like in omelets or schmeared on little toasts.

Serves 4

CREAMY CRAB RANGOON SQUASH BLOSSOMS

Make the crab filling:

In a stand mixer fitted with a paddle attachment or in a large bowl with a hand mixer or spoon, mix the cream and mascarpone cheeses until smooth and light. Add the shallot, soy sauce, and salt and mix until well combined. Gently fold in the crabmeat and almonds. Season with salt to taste.

Make the chive yogurt:

In a blender, combine the cream and chives until smooth. In a medium bowl, whisk the mixture into the yogurt and season with salt.

Make the vinaigrette:

In a small bowl, whisk together the lemon juice, soy sauce, olive oil, red pepper flakes, syrup, and garlic.

Using a piping bag or a plastic zippered bag with a corner snipped off, fill the squash blossoms three-fourths of the way to the edge with the crab filling. Chill in the refrigerator for at least 1 hour and up to 1 day before frying.

FILLING

1 pound cream cheese, at room temperature

8 ounces mascarpone cheese

1½ tablespoons minced shallot

½ tablespoon soy sauce

½ teaspoon kosher salt, plus more to taste

8 ounces picked-through lump crabmeat

½ cup sliced almonds, toasted

CHIVE YOGURT

¼ cup heavy cream

¼ cup chopped chives

8 ounces plain Greek yogurt

½ teaspoon kosher salt

VINAIGRETTE

¼ cup fresh lemon juice

2 tablespoons soy sauce

¼ cup full-bodied olive oil

1½ teaspoons crushed red pepper flakes

1 teaspoon maple syrup

1 garlic clove, minced

8 to 10 medium squash blossoms

2 cups cornstarch

2 cups all-purpose flour

12 ounces cold beer

⅓ cup sliced almonds, toasted

In a large pot over medium-high heat, heat the canola oil to 375°F.

In a shallow bowl, whisk together the cornstarch and flour. Gently mix in the beer with a fork, being careful not to over-mix so the beer stays carbonated.

Dunk the stuffed blossoms in the beer batter one at a time, making sure to evenly and smoothly coat the flowers. Carefully drop the blossoms into the oil, working in batches if necessary not to crowd the pot, and fry for 1 minute or until golden. Gently agitate the squash blossoms while frying to ensure they cook evenly.

Spread the chive yogurt on the bottom of a platter and arrange the fried blossoms over the yogurt. Drizzle with the vinaigrette, sprinkle with almonds, and serve immediately.

If there were a list of things that people get most excited about when they first come into season, soft-shell crabs would definitely be on it. They're just as sweet and delicious as hard-shell crabs, but you can actually eat the shells (which means a lot less work to get to all that crabby goodness). I like dredging them in a really light tempura batter and frying them, so they're crispy but not smothered in breading. Then you just dunk the whole thing in sauce and get messy with it. Serve 'em up with Sweet Corn Elotes (page 193), and call it the perfect summer meal. *Serves 4*

SOFT-SHELL CRAB
IN CHILE SAUCE

Make the chile sauce:

In a small bowl, whisk together the tamarind, ketchup, hot sauce, fish sauce, rice wine, pickle liquid, soy sauce, sesame oil, habanero sauce, garlic, and ginger. Add 2 tablespoons water. In a medium saucepot over medium-high heat, combine the chile sauce mixture, stock, and butter. Bring to a simmer and cook for 2 to 3 minutes. By heating the sauce you better incorporate the butter without the risk of the ingredients separating. Keep warm while the crab fries.

Heat the oil in a large pot to 375°F.

In a shallow bowl, whisk together the cornstarch and flour. Gently mix in the beer with a fork, being careful not to over-mix so the beer stays carbonated.

Split the crabs down the center so that the two sets of legs are separate. Dunk the crab in the batter and carefully add it to the oil, working in batches so you don't crowd the pot. Fry for 2 minutes, or until golden and crisp. Gently agitate so the crab fries evenly.

Serve the crab drizzled with chile oil, garnished with strawberries, and with the chile sauce alongside.

CHILE SAUCE

⅓ cup tamarind pulp, or 2 tablespoons tamarind paste

¼ cup ketchup

¼ cup smoky hot sauce of the chipotle variety

2 tablespoons fish sauce

2 tablespoons Shaoxing rice wine or dry sherry

2 tablespoons brine from Pickled Red Onions (page 258)

1½ tablespoons soy sauce

1 tablespoon toasted sesame oil

1 tablespoon sweet habanero hot sauce

1 garlic clove, minced

½ teaspoon minced fresh ginger

½ cup vegetable stock

2 tablespoons unsalted butter

2 quarts canola oil, for frying

2 cups cornstarch

2 cups all-purpose flour

12 ounces cold beer

4 soft-shell crabs, cleaned

Chile oil

6 strawberries, hulled and thinly sliced

TIP

When it comes to buying soft-shell crab, here are a few important things to consider: First, never buy frozen. Second, have your fishmonger clean them for you (meaning they're trimmed just behind the eyes and in front of the tail, and the lungs are removed). Make sure the crabs were alive up until when they were cleaned—it makes a ton of difference in the quality and flavor. And plan on eating them the day they're cleaned, or they won't taste as fresh.

1 cup Szechuan Chile Sauce (page 127)

½ cup blueberry jam, homemade (see page 134) or store-bought

1- to 2-pound skin-on salmon fillet, any pin bones removed

Canola oil

Kosher salt and pepper

¼ cup torn fresh basil leaves

¼ cup torn fresh mint leaves

I'm not going to be that chef who's all in your grill about using only produce or animal products that you grow or raise yourself on your own fancy biodynamic farm. But as I said before, there are some times when buying good quality makes all the difference. Salmon is one of those things: not all salmon is created equal. That sad, pale stuff at the grocery store? That's giving salmon a bad name. High-quality, wild-caught salmon—like Copper River sockeye when it's in season—is the way salmon should be: bright orange and meaty, not slimy, pale, or fishy. And the skin is super-tasty, too. I love showcasing this beautiful fish by taking a big hunk, throwing it on the grill, and serving it with Szechuan Chile Sauce plus a secret ingredient: blueberry jam. I know it might sound weird to put jam in your chile sauce, but trust me on this. The fruit brings together all the flavors of this dish with its subtle acidity and sweetness. Finish this off with a batch of grilled veggies and you've got a meal. *Serves 4 to 6*

GRILLED SALMON
WITH BLUEBERRY-SZECHUAN CHILE SAUCE

Preheat a grill or grill pan so it's nice and hot. To grill the fish without its falling apart, the grill grates need to heat for at least 15 minutes before you start cooking.

Whisk together the chile sauce and blueberry jam.

Lightly coat both sides of the salmon with the oil and season with salt and pepper. Gently put the fish on the grill, skin side down. Cook until the skin crisps, 5 to 7 minutes, then use a long-handled metal spatula to gently scrape the skin free of the grates before flipping. Releasing the skin will help the entire fillet to flip without breaking. Carefully flip the fish and continue cooking on the flesh side until medium to medium rare, 1 to 2 more minutes. Transfer the salmon to a platter, skin side down.

Drizzle the fish with a healthy amount of the sauce, and garnish with the herbs. Serve family style.

The collar of hamachi (also known as yellowtail)—the section just below the head and gills—is often tossed as scraps. It sometimes seems like there's more bone and cartilage than meat, but those in the know save this scrumptious cut. I particularly like to shellac the collar with a Japanese mash-up marinade inspired by the sweet unagi glaze that comes on eel sushi. Soy and mirin are reduced to a maple syrup–like consistency and given a little acidity with lime. If you can't find hamachi, salmon or halibut collar can do in a pinch. In summer, local tomatoes and peaches are in season at the same time, so they should definitely be hanging out together. Just be sure you're buying slightly under-ripe peaches because you want a little crunch and acidity. *Serves 6 to 8*

1 cup soy sauce

1 cup mirin

½ cup soju or vodka

1 cup sugar

6 to 8 hamachi collars

⅔ cup mayonnaise

1 tablespoon fresh lime juice

2 small apricots, pitted and sliced thin

2 plums, pitted and thinly sliced

1 large under-ripe peach, pitted and sliced thin

2 medium heirloom tomatoes, diced

1 pint Sun Gold or heirloom cherry tomatoes, halved

1 tablespoon chopped fresh sorrel

1 tablespoon chopped fresh cilantro

1 tablespoon chopped fresh basil

¼ cup fresh mint leaves, torn

HAMACHI COLLAR
WITH UNAGI MAYO AND HEIRLOOM SALAD

Combine the soy sauce, mirin, soju, and sugar in a medium saucepan and whisk to combine. Simmer over low heat until thickened, about 40 minutes. Remove the pan from the heat and allow the sauce to cool fully before using.

Preheat the grill to medium-high heat.

Pour half of the marinade (about 1½ cups) into a shallow dish and marinate the collars about 10 minutes, turning once. Reserve the rest of the marinade.

While the hamachi marinates, assemble the salad. Whisk together the mayonnaise and lime juice in a medium bowl. Then whisk in almost all of the remaining marinade until the mixture is smooth and has no visible mayonnaise specks. Reserve a small amount of marinade for when the fish comes off the grill.

Toss together the apricots, plums, peach, tomatoes, sorrel, cilantro, and basil and dress with about two-thirds of the dressing. Transfer to a platter.

Grill the fish, turning once, until the flesh begins to firm, 20 to 25 minutes. In the last minute of cooking, brush all sides of the fish with the rest of the marinade. Arrange the hot fish collars on top of the salad, drizzle with the rest of the dressing, and garnish with mint. Pick the collars off with your fingers as you eat.

VINAIGRETTE

2 tablespoons soy sauce, plus more to taste

½ tablespoon fish sauce

¾ teaspoon seasoned rice wine vinegar

¾ teaspoon toasted sesame oil

¾ teaspoon crushed red pepper flakes, preferably Korean, or to taste

¾ teaspoon dark brown sugar

1 small shallot, sliced thin

1 large garlic clove, minced

½ tablespoon minced fresh ginger

1 ounce or 8 whole perilla (sesame) or shiso leaves (essential—no other leaves work in this recipe)

2 tablespoons extra-virgin olive oil

Salt, if needed

MUSSELS

1 tablespoon extra-virgin olive oil

2 shallots, sliced thin

½ bulb fennel, sliced thin

Kosher salt

4 garlic cloves, sliced thin

2 sprigs of fresh thyme

2 cups dry white wine

2 pounds mussels, scrubbed and debearded (discard any mussels still open after tapping gently)

8 tablespoons (1 stick) unsalted butter

¼ cup toasted bread crumbs

There have been different versions of a mussels dish on the menu at Girl & the Goat every year for six years, but this one is my favorite. The idea came back with one of my sous chefs after she spent some time in Korea. There, they marinate perilla leaves—which are similar to shiso and have kind of an anise taste—in sesame oil, soy sauce, and chiles. Then they spoon them over rice, just like that. It's super tasty, so we turned it into a vinaigrette that we use to steam mussels. Then we finish it off with some butter (okay, a lot of butter) and serve it with crusty bread. Jamie Bissonnette taught me how to eat mussels: you use one of the empty shell pairs like tongs to pluck out all the other mussels. Genius! *Serves 2*

MUSSELS FOR TWO
WITH MARINATED PERILLA VINAIGRETTE

Make the vinaigrette:

In a large container, combine 2 tablespoons water with the soy sauce, fish sauce, vinegar, sesame oil, red pepper flakes, brown sugar, shallot, garlic, ginger, and perilla leaves. Mix well and make sure the leaves are fully submerged. Let them marinate at room temperature for at least 1 hour or as long as 12 hours.

Put the mixture into a blender and pulse until the ingredients are blended but the sauce still has a lot of texture. Transfer the mixture to a medium bowl and whisk in the olive oil. Adjust the seasoning with additional soy sauce and salt, if desired.

Make the mussels:

In a 3- to 4-quart Dutch oven or heavy-bottomed pot, heat the olive oil over medium until shimmering. Add the shallots and fennel, and season with salt. Sauté until both are translucent, 5 to 7 minutes. Add the garlic and thyme, and cook until fragrant and wilted, about 1 minute. Pour in the wine and bring to a boil.

Add the vinaigrette, mussels, and butter, stirring once or twice so that the aromatics are well distributed. Cover the pot with a lid and reduce the heat so the liquid simmers. Cook until the mussels open, 8 to 10 minutes. Without removing the lid, shake the pot once or twice during cooking to prevent burning. Once done, discard any mussels that have not opened.

Serve the mussels in the pot or transfer to a serving dish. Drizzle generously with the pan juices, and then sprinkle the bread crumbs on top.

You can make this fried fish either whole or as fillets. I like frying a cleaned whole fish, which makes a dramatic presentation when you have people over—plus, the whole fish kind of opens up in the fryer, making a perfect little well for pouring in a bacon sweet-and-sour-sauce. That said, fillets are just as tasty! Yellowtail snapper, red snapper, black bass, or barramundi are all great for this recipe. (The only fish I would avoid using are oily ones like salmon or tuna.) I like to fry fish with a light beer tempura batter. It comes out crisp, light, and not at all greasy. The trick is to use half cornstarch and half flour, so the batter gets crispy; also, use ice-cold beer, which makes the tempura flaky. The hoisin mayo is a really simple dipper that you can easily throw together, but it has a totally addictive "special sauce" flavor that is great not only on crispy fish but also on just about any sandwich.

Serves 4

CRISPY WHOLE FISH
WITH BACON SWEET 'N' SOUR AND HOISIN MAYO

Make the sauce:

In a medium saucepan over medium-low heat, render the bacon until crisp, about 8 minutes. Add the onion and garlic, and cook in the bacon fat until soft, about 5 minutes. Pour in the vinegar and use your spoon to scrape up any brown bits from the bottom. Add the pineapple, pineapple juice, tomatoes, lime juice, fish sauce, brown sugar, and sambal oelek, and cook over medium-low heat for 25 to 30 minutes. The sauce should thicken significantly.

Make the hoisin mayo:

In a medium bowl, whisk together the mayo and hoisin sauce.

Fry the fish:

Pour the oil into a large pot and heat to 375°F.

Meanwhile, in a small saucepan over medium-low heat, heat the bacon sauce with the butter.

SAUCE

8 ounces sliced bacon, cut crosswise into ¼-inch-thick pieces

½ cup minced sweet onion

1 tablespoon minced garlic

¼ cup malt vinegar

½ fresh pineapple, diced small (3 to 4 cups), with ½ cup juice

½ cup canned diced tomatoes

¼ cup fresh lime juice

¼ cup fish sauce

⅓ cup brown sugar

1 tablespoon sambal oelek

HOISIN MAYO

1 cup Kewpie mayo, or other store-bought variety

¼ cup hoisin sauce, homemade (page 67) or store-bought

FISH

4 quarts canola oil, for deep-frying

3 tablespoons unsalted butter

2 cups cornstarch

2 cups all-purpose flour

12 ounces cold beer

2 (1½- to 2-pound) whole sea bass, head, tail, and skin on; cleaned and boned

Chopped scallion greens, for garnish

(Continues)

In a shallow bowl, combine the cornstarch and flour. Lightly coat the fish—inside and out if you're frying a whole one—with the mixture and set aside. Gently mix the beer into the remaining flour mixture with a fork, taking care not to over-mix so the beer stays carbonated. The batter should be thin enough that if you dip your finger in it, you can see through the batter.

Dredge one fish (or fish fillet) at a time in the tempura batter, ensuring that it's fully and evenly coated. Carefully drop the fish into the hot oil and cook until the fish is golden brown and the flesh is firm, 7 to 8 minutes. Repeat with the second fish or remaining fillets.

Spread the warm bacon sauce onto a long serving platter or shallow bowl. Lay the fried fish over the top, drizzle with the hoisin mayo, and garnish with scallions.

GOOD STUFF: KEWPIE MAYO

This store-bought Japanese mayonnaise is my favorite. It's got a tangy zip like Miracle Whip (which I grew up on), and you'll want to put it on every sandwich you make. You can find it in almost any Asian market.

1 tablespoon minced garlic

3 tablespoons sambal oelek

1½ cups canola oil

½ pound extra-large
(26/30 count) shrimp,
peeled (save the shells)
and deveined

BROTH

Canola oil

1 cup diced fennel bulb

1 cup diced yellow onion

2 garlic cloves, smashed

1 (2-inch) piece galangal,
chopped into chunks

½ stalk lemongrass, split
lengthwise

1 (1-inch) piece fresh
ginger, peeled and
chopped into chunks

½ teaspoon mustard seeds

½ teaspoon fennel seeds

¼ teaspoon black
peppercorns

1 dried Thai chile

¼ cup dry white wine

1 cup canned diced
tomatoes, drained

¼ cup canned shrimp paste
(found in Asian markets
or in the international
aisle)

1 tablespoon tomato paste

2 tablespoons brandy or
whiskey

¼ cup cream of coconut

2 teaspoons fish sauce

2 tablespoons fresh lime
juice

I owe this invention to one of my sous chefs, Boo, who loves the traditional French fish stew bouillabaisse, but also finds it's often missing some excitement. Then he thought about *tom kah*, a Thai soup that has all these spicy and sour layers with coconut milk and lime juice, and figured, *Why not combine the two?* That's how I roll, too—adding Asian flair to classic European dishes to amp up their flavor. The end result is a rich, complex-tasting stew that's made with almost whatever fish looks good at the market (just not the oilier types like salmon or tuna). Just be sure to get some mussels or clams in there, since they are what give the broth lots of seafood flavor. Serve it as a simple soup or do it like we do at the diner and serve it over a big pile of mashed potatoes.

Serves 4

THAI-STYLE BOUILLABAISSE

Marinate the shrimp:
In a small bowl, whisk together the garlic, sambal oelek, and oil. Pour the mixture over the shrimp and let marinate in the refrigerator for at least 1 hour and up to 2 days.

Make the broth:
Add just enough oil to the bottom of a large stockpot to coat. Over medium heat, sweat the fennel, onion, and garlic until soft, 5 minutes. Add the galangal, lemongrass, ginger, mustard seeds, fennel seeds, peppercorns, and chile. Cook for 2 minutes. Deglaze with the wine, scraping up any brown bits from the bottom of the pan with your spoon, and reduce the wine until almost completely evaporated, 5 minutes.

Stir in the tomatoes, shrimp paste, tomato paste, and brandy and cook for 2 more minutes.

Add the reserved shrimp shells and 8 cups water. Bring to a boil, then reduce the heat so that the liquid simmers very gently. Cover the pot and cook for 1 hour.

(Continues)

FISH AND MUSSELS

Canola oil

1 pound skinless whitefish fillet, sliced into 1-inch pieces

Kosher salt

2 tablespoons unsalted butter

½ cup cherry tomatoes

¼ cup sliced yellow onion

1 pound mussels, scrubbed and debearded (discard any that stay open after gentle tapping)

2 tablespoons minced fresh sorrel

2 tablespoons torn fresh cilantro leaves

Strain the mixture into a large bowl and let cool completely. Discard the solids. Stir in the coconut cream, fish sauce, and lime juice. Transfer the broth to a small pot and heat until almost boiling.

Cook the fish:
Add enough oil to a large sauté pan with a fitted lid to coat the bottom. Over medium-high heat, add the marinated shrimp and cook, turning once, until bright pink and firm, 4 to 5 minutes. Remove the shrimp from the pan.

Season the fish with salt. In the same sauté pan, adding more oil if necessary, cook the fish over medium-high heat until the flesh is firm and flakey, 4 minutes, turning once. Remove the fish from the pan.

Add the butter, cherry tomatoes, and onion and cook over medium-high heat for 2 minutes. Add the mussels and 1 cup of the broth. Cover the pan with the lid and steam the mussels until they open, about 6 minutes. Discard any mussels that don't open during that time. Add the cooked shrimp and fish to the pan and cook for 1 more minute.

Distribute the broth, fish, and mussels among 4 bowls. Garnish each with some of the sorrel and cilantro and serve.

Clams with fermented black beans is a classic Chinese dish that's super-delicious but can get kind of salty and intense. To balance and mellow things out, I add tarragon-garlic-sambal butter, which I also use on everything from bread to mussel dishes (adding it at the end to the broth makes an awesome sauce). After the clam shells have opened, we stir in the butter, and sometimes add Fresno chiles for extra spice. *Serves 4*

STEAMED CLAMS
IN TARRAGON BUTTER

Make the tarragon butter:
In a medium bowl, beat the butter with a spoon or spatula until light and fluffy, about 1 minute. Add the tarragon, ginger, garlic, soy sauce, and sambal oelek, and mix until well combined.

Cook the clams:
In a large pot over medium heat, render the bacon until it's almost crisp, about 8 minutes. Add the celery and onion, and sweat them for 2 to 3 minutes. Add the clams and toss to coat. Add the rice wine, lemon zest, and tarragon butter. Cover the pot and steam the clams until they open, about 5 minutes. Discard any that do not open.

Transfer the clams and their cooking liquid to a large bowl and sprinkle with the scallions and cilantro. Serve hot.

TARRAGON BUTTER

- 8 tablespoons (1 stick) unsalted butter, at room temperature
- 1 tablespoon chopped fresh tarragon
- ½ teaspoon minced fresh ginger
- 1 teaspoon minced garlic
- ½ tablespoon soy sauce
- ½ tablespoon sambal oelek

CLAMS

- 4 strips of bacon, sliced into ¼-inch pieces (¼ cup)
- ¼ cup thinly sliced celery
- ¼ cup thinly sliced onion
- 2 to 3 pounds littleneck clams, soaked in cold water and well scrubbed
- ½ cup Shaoxing rice wine
- 2 tablespoons grated lemon zest
- ¼ cup chopped scallions (green and white parts)
- 2 tablespoons fresh cilantro leaves, roughly chopped

CINCO DE MAYO
Fish Edition

. . . .

In Chicago, making it through the winter to spring is reason enough to celebrate! After those long, cold months, everyone's ready to get outside and enjoy the sunshine. No matter when May 5 falls, Gary and I make the following Sunday a day of food, outside-ness, and good times. Also, let's be honest: A Cinco de Mayo party is just an excuse to have a bunch of people over and drink micheladas or margaritas (or our fun spin, the Modus Mandarita), right? So if you're going to do it, you might as well offer a new take on the expected. For example, instead of going straight for the ground beef, pork, and chicken for your tacos and tostadas, try fish!

Cinco de Mayo is also, for me, a great way to take advantage of the fact that every day at Little Goat we turn out enough fresh tortillas and masa chips to feed a small army. They are so easy to make and *so* much better than anything you'd buy at the grocery store. I'm still trying to figure out how we could sell our chips by the bag—they're that good. Because they're fried while they're still fresh, they stay crisp longer, even when heaped with mounds of dips like Pimiento Cheese (page 168) and Avocado Smash (page 169).

This is definitely the kind of party for which you can put out all the different components and let people pile up their own plates. As long as you're giving them options for sauces and textures, everyone will end up with layers and layers of great flavor. Oh, and don't forget the Choco Taco Sundaes (page 177) for something sweet. Because, obviously.

Gary put Ska brewing's Modus Mandarina IPA on the Duck Duck Goat menu, and it easily became one of my favorites. It's brewed with fresh orange peel and also made with mandarina hops, which add even more citrus notes. Our bar team created this cocktail as a fun nod to the margarita, adding a pineapple–Fresno chile "shrub," a play on a sweet drinking vinegar but using the brine from pickled Fresnos instead of vinegar. And, of course, tequila. *Serves 4*

MODUS MANDARITA

In a small bowl, mix the sugar and ¾ cup water to make a simple syrup. Stir until dissolved. Combine with the pineapple juice and pickle liquid.

Rim four tumblers with coarse salt and set aside.

Shake the tequila, pineapple juice mixture, and lime juice together with ice. Strain over fresh ice into the prepared tumblers. Top each glass with 1 ounce (2 tablespoons) beer. Serve with sliced pickled chiles and lime wedges, if using.

¾ cup sugar

⅓ cup strained pineapple juice

⅔ cup brine from Pickled Fresno Chiles (page 263), plus sliced chiles for serving (optional)

Coarse salt, for rimming the glasses

8 ounces silver tequila, preferably Peligroso

3 ounces (6 tablespoons) fresh lime juice, plus lime wedges for serving (optional)

Crushed ice

4 ounces (8 tablespoons) Modus Mandarina Beer or other citrus-based beer

2 quarts canola oil, for
    frying

½ cup masa flour

⅛ teaspoon kosher salt, plus
    more for seasoning

I made fresh chips for the first time back when Girl &
the Goat opened and I entered a chili cook-off. I wanted
something fun and crunchy to sprinkle on top, so one of my
cooks, David Avila, taught us how to make fresh masa chips.
My team won, and I've been making them ever since. We
serve them two ways at the diner: either as rounds (which are
perfect for making tostadas) or broken up into chips.

Don't get me wrong, I also love fried corn tortillas—or
really good store-bought chips—but these have the best
texture and flavor. And they take only three ingredients—
masa flour, water, and salt! (Just be sure to get the Maseca
brand of masa flour.)

Since it's not a Cinco de Mayo party without chips and
dip, serve your masa chips with two of my favorites: Pimiento
Cheese (page 168) and Avocado Smash (page 169). Or load
them up with tostada toppings (see page 170). Don't forget
to save some for the Choco Taco Sundaes on page 177!

Makes 8 (3-inch) masa rounds or about 4 cups chips

MASA CHIPS
AND DIPS

In a large pot, heat the oil to 325°F.

In a medium bowl, using your hands, mix the corn flour, salt, and
6 tablespoons lukewarm water until a soft ball forms. Let the
dough rest for 3 to 5 minutes.

Put 2 tablespoons of the dough into a zippered bag and flatten
it using a tortilla press or rolling pin. The dough rounds should
be 1/16 inch thick or 3 inches in diameter. For tostadas, keep the
round whole. For chips, cut the round into quarters. Fry the
rounds in the hot oil, turning once, until golden, 3 minutes per
side. While still hot, season with salt. The tostadas will stick
together if the fryer is crowed, so cooking them one at a time is
recommended; chips can be fried in small batches, agitating with
tongs to keep them from sticking.

The first time I had this, I had no idea what a bunch of cheddar cheese was doing swimming in mayonnaise with bits of red bell pepper floating in it. Traditional southern dish or not, it seemed straight-up *weird* . . . but really, really tasty. My version is a little more integrated and super-creamy with cream cheese, mayo, cheddar, and pimientos. Don't try to make this with pre-shredded, not-so-great cheese or it won't whip into the rest of the ingredients (though finely shredded extra-sharp cheddar will work, too).

Admittedly, this dip has absolutely nothing to do with Cinco de Mayo, but it's seriously addictive with masa chips. And it is great as a spread on sandwiches, in omelets, or heaped on English muffins, bagels, or crackers—pretty much anything. *Makes 5 cups*

1 pound cream cheese, at room temperature

2 pounds sharp cheddar cheese, finely shredded (6 cups)

¾ cup mayonnaise

1 (11.5-ounce) can pimientos, drained and chopped

Kosher salt

PIMIENTO CHEESE

In the bowl of a stand mixer with the paddle attachment or in a large bowl with a hand mixer or spoon, beat the cream cheese until completely smooth. Mix in the cheddar cheese, mayonnaise, and pimientos until fully incorporated. Season with salt to taste. Serve right away or cover and store in the fridge for up to 1 week.

2 ripe Hass avocados

2 teaspoons fresh lemon juice

¼ teaspoon kosher salt

I love avocados so much that I never do much more to them than add a little salt, pepper, and lemon juice—a super-simple guacamole. Everyone always asks me how I pick the best avocados, so I'll give you the secret: Be that person who touches and squeezes every single one in the pile. You want to be able to *just* squeeze the skin. And forget the organic ones—I'm not sure why, but their texture is never quite as good. *Makes 2 cups*

AVOCADO SMASH

Cut the avocados in half and discard the pits. Using the tip of a paring knife, score the avocado flesh into medium squares. Use a large spoon to scoop out the cubes into a bowl and add the lemon juice and salt. Mix, smashing gently with a fork or spoon. The dip should be chunky and well combined.

In my world, *tostada* is really just Spanish for "yummy stuff piled on a big round chip." For this version, I pair the richness of avocado with shrimp that's been tossed in a creamy but lightly spiced dressing, plus a simple cabbage slaw punctuated with tangy pickled peppers and onions. There are two tricks to cooking great shrimp: butterflying them—or slicing them almost completely halfway through—and marinating them just before cooking. They get a ton of flavor, inside and out, and cook quickly, which means they can keep their nice, firm texture and not get rubbery. No one wants to eat a shrimp you can bounce off the floor!

Makes 8 tostadas

SHRIMP TOSTADAS

Marinate the shrimp:
In a medium bowl, whisk together the oil, sambal oelek, and garlic. Toss in the shrimp to coat and marinate in the fridge for 1 hour.

Heat a large nonstick sauté pan over high heat. Add the shrimp and sear for 2 minutes without tossing. Cook for another 3 minutes, tossing, until the shrimp is bright orange and opaque. Transfer the shrimp to a sheet pan and allow them to cool completely.

In a medium bowl, whisk together the mayonnaise, lemon juice, and sauce. When the shrimp are cool, toss them in the flavored mayo to coat.

Mix the slaw:
In a large bowl, whisk together the vinegar, sugar, salt, and olive oil. Add the cabbage, pickled onions, and cilantro and toss to coat.

Build the tostadas:
Divide the avocado mash evenly among the masa rounds. Top each tostada with the dressed shrimp, a handful of the cabbage salad, and a sprinkle of the pickled peppers.

SHRIMP

1½ cups canola oil

3 tablespoons sambal oelek

1 tablespoon minced garlic

1½ pounds extra-large (26/30 count) shrimp, peeled, deveined, and butterflied

½ cup mayonnaise

2¼ teaspoons fresh lemon juice

1¼ tablespoons Kimchi Sauce (page 259)

SLAW

2½ tablespoons red wine vinegar

½ teaspoon sugar

Small pinch of salt

1 tablespoon extra-virgin olive oil

2 cups shredded green cabbage

¼ cup Pickled Red Onions (page 258)

2 tablespoons fresh cilantro leaves

TOSTADAS

Avocado Smash (page 169)

Masa Chips (page 167), formed and fried as tostadas

⅓ cup Pickled Hungarian Hots and Bananas (page 262)

4 cups all-purpose flour,
plus more for rolling

5 tablespoons unsalted
butter, at room
temperature

2 teaspoons kosher salt

2 teaspoons baking powder

On our honeymoon in Belize, we discovered a thicker, fluffier, richer style of tortilla that's traditional there. We had them with just about every meal (even breakfast—hello, tortilla and jam!), and when I got home, I had to learn how to re-create their chewy, doughy goodness. I bought a Belizean cookbook, tinkered with things a bit, and now have a version that I use at the diner for our tacos and quesadillas. Is making your own tortillas an extra step that you could skip in favor of store-bought? Absolutely. But it's easy to do and totally worth it. Plus, you can freeze the tortillas in small stacks in plastic zippered bags and pull them out whenever the taco mood strikes. Before serving, I reheat them in a dry pan over medium heat, warming them for 1 minute on each side.

Makes 15 flour tortillas

FRESH FLOUR TORTILLAS

Put a pizza stone in the oven and preheat to 425°F.

In the bowl of a stand mixer fitted with the paddle attachment or in a large bowl with a hand mixer or spoon, mix the flour, butter, salt, and baking powder with 1 cup water until the butter is just incorporated. The dough should be shaggy, not smooth.

Turn out the dough onto a floured surface. Cut the dough into 15 equal pieces. Roll each piece into a ball about the size of a golf ball. Let the dough rest for 5 minutes, then roll it flat into 1/16-inch-thick tortillas.

Working in batches, transfer the tortillas to the pizza stone. Cook for 30 seconds to 1 minute, then flip when the raw side begins to bubble. Cook for 30 seconds more and remove from the oven. Repeat until all are cooked.

Halibut has great, clean flavor and a really meaty texture. I often give it a quick dip in Sauce Green (page 133) for a little marinade action, which coats the fish nicely, adds lots of flavor, and lends the whole thing a fun, festive color. In addition to homemade tortillas, I put out a bright pickled rhubarb relish that has just enough sugar in the pickling liquid to balance the natural pucker factor of the rhubarb. Just remember that not all Serrano chiles are created equal—add them to the mix a little bit at a time to make sure you're not going overboard with the spice. *Makes 8 tacos*

HALIBUT TACOS

In a medium bowl, whisk together the pickling liquid and olive oil. Stir in the pickled rhubarb, onion, scallions, chile, and mint.

Heat the canola oil in a large nonstick sauté pan over high heat. Season the fish with salt and carefully add to the pan, working in batches if necessary. Sear, turning once, until lightly browned, 5 minutes on each side. Remove the fish from the pan and break it into large chunks.

Distribute the halibut evenly among the tortillas and dress with the pickled rhubarb relish.

¼ cup brine from Pickled Rhubarb (page 265)

1 tablespoon extra-virgin olive oil

2 cups Pickled Rhubarb (page 265), chopped

¼ cup small diced red onion

¼ cup thinly sliced scallions (green and white parts)

1 tablespoon thinly sliced Serrano chile

1 tablespoon roughly chopped fresh mint

1 tablespoon canola oil

2 pounds skinless halibut fillet

Kosher salt

8 flour tortillas, homemade (page 173) or store-bought

CANDIED PEPITAS

1 tablespoon egg white
(about ½ large egg white)

½ cup sugar

2 cups raw pepitas
(pumpkin seeds)

Pinch of kosher salt

Pinch of cayenne pepper

SUNDAES

1 cup milk chocolate chips

6 Masa Chips (page 167)

2 cups semi-sweet
chocolate chips

¾ cup coconut oil

Sour Cream Ice Cream
(recipe follows)

½ cup cajeta, homemade
(page 249) or
store-bought

Whipped cream, for serving

There was a time when Taco Bell offered a dessert by the same name: a chocolate-coated waffle-cone taco shell filled with ice cream and these crunchy little cookie things. One day I was sitting on an airplane, thinking about dessert—as one does—and my mind went to the Choco Taco. Then I thought, *Huh? We make our own masa chips, and they're awesome. Why not dip them in chocolate?* And the rest is history—a nacho-style dessert with sour cream ice cream (or vanilla, if you're going the store-bought route), plus cajeta (or goat's milk caramel) and a chocolate drizzle that creates a "Magic Shell." You could also skip the whole sundae situation and just eat the chocolate-dipped masa chips. *Makes 6 sundaes*

CHOCO TACO SUNDAES

Make the candied pepitas:
Preheat the oven to 300°F and line a sheet pan with parchment paper.

Whip the egg white with the sugar until slightly frothy. Add the pepitas, salt, and cayenne. Mix until the pepitas are well coated, then turn them out onto the prepared sheet pan. Bake until the seeds are lightly browned, 12 to 15 minutes. Cool before breaking them apart into small pieces.

Make the sundaes:
Line a large sheet pan with parchment paper.

Melt the milk chocolate chips in a small bowl in the microwave, pulsing in 10-second installments, or in a double boiler over hot water until smooth.

Dunk the masa chips in the melted chocolate so they're almost completely coated. Lay them on the lined sheet pan and refrigerate immediately. Chill until the chocolate has set, about 10 minutes.

Melt the semi-sweet chocolate chips and coconut oil together in a small bowl in the microwave, pulsing in 10-second installments, or in the top of a double boiler over hot water until well incorporated.

Scoop the ice cream into bowls, drizzle with the chocolate sauce, dollop with cajeta and whipped cream, and sprinkle with several chocolate-dipped masa chips. Serve immediately.

Sour Cream Ice Cream

Makes 1 quart

2½ cups half-and-half

⅔ cup sugar

⅛ teaspoon kosher salt

6 large egg yolks

½ cup sour cream

In a large saucepan over low heat, bring the half-and-half, sugar, and salt to a simmer until the sugar dissolves, about 5 minutes. Remove from the heat.

In a medium bowl, whisk the yolks until smooth. Continuing to whisk constantly, slowly add about one-third of the hot half-and-half mixture to the yolks. Whisk the yolk mixture back into the pot with the remaining half-and-half.

Return the pot to medium-low heat and cook gently, stirring with a wooden spoon, until the mixture thickens and coats the back of the spoon, 5 to 6 minutes,. Strain through a fine-mesh strainer into a bowl set over ice cubes and water. Let the mixture cool to room temperature before whisking in the sour cream. Cover and chill for at least 4 hours or overnight.

Follow the instructions on the machine to churn the ice cream. Transfer to a covered container and freeze for at least 1 hour before serving, or store up to 1 month in the freezer.

VEGGIES ARE FUN, TOO!

GOAT-O GOAT-O SALAD *183*

KOHLRABI SALAD
with Ginger-Maple Dressing *184*

TOFU NOODLE SALAD
with Fermented Tofu Vinaigrette *187*

**BABY CARROT
GIARDINIERA** *188*

ROASTED BEET SALAD
with Pomelo Relish *191*

RAPINI RELISH *192*

SWEET CORN ELOTES *193*

**ROASTED SHISHITO
PEPPERS**
with Sesame Miso and Parmesan *195*

**PAN-ROASTED
CAULIFLOWER**
with Pickled Peppers *197*

SWEET POTATO GRATIN
with Blue Cheese Dressing
and Crispy Onions *199*

MUSHROOM RAGOUT *203*

Farmers' Market Picnic

Strawberry Gazpacho *207*

Eggplant Zaalouk *208*

Marinated Sweet Cherries
with Whipped Feta *211*

Green Goddess
Chicken Salad *212*

WHEN I WAS OPENING GIRL & THE GOAT, I DECIDED TO HAVE A section of the menu devoted to vegetables—and it made me nervous. I mean, I eat vegetables, and I like vegetables, but I was worried about finding ways to make them *interesting*. I wanted to celebrate them, show them off. Over time, I've figured out how to make vegetables as special as any other part of the meal; I've even converted Gary, who straight-up didn't like them before we met.

Many of us grew up eating steamed-to-mush frozen vegetables that maybe got tossed in margarine or Velveeta. But when fresh, in-season vegetables get cooked right, they have about a million times more flavor than frozen ones. So if you think you don't like vegetables, think again. Once you've got great raw materials, the trick is pairing them with the right flavors. Think about corn: it's naturally sweet, so adding a little bit of saltiness and maybe a little acid helps round out its flavor. Earthy beets call out for bright citrus. You want to fill in the gaps of what a vegetable's missing while still highlighting its natural veg-ness.

DRESSING

½ cup roasted and salted peanuts

1 garlic clove

1 Thai chile

¼ cup fish sauce

¼ cup tamarind paste

¼ cup malt vinegar

2 tablespoons fresh lime juice

1½ teaspoons dark brown sugar

½ cup canola oil

Kosher salt

SALAD

8 cups leafy lettuce (preferably Red Oakleaf lettuce), washed, root end trimmed, leaves torn into pieces

3 medium carrots, sliced very thin

3 spring onions, sliced thin (white and green parts)

1 small cucumber, peeled and sliced very thin

2 firm peaches, pitted and sliced thin

1 medium or 2 small kohlrabi, peeled and sliced thin

1½ cups halved Sun Gold or heirloom cherry tomatoes

¼ cup fresh mint leaves, torn

¼ cup fresh basil leaves, torn

½ cup roasted and salted peanuts, roughly chopped

This is a play on Malaysian *gado gado*, which literally means "mix mix": a pile of veggies in a big bowl topped with a peanut vinaigrette and a sprinkling of peanuts for a little crunch. I love going to the market or the garden and grabbing whatever looks nice—baby carrots, sugar snap peas, Sun Gold tomatoes, peaches; then I make it look pretty, put it on the table, and let people mix it up. This vinaigrette is my take on the original, a balanced and bright, slightly less sweet version that's perfect for a summer salad or even just some sliced cucumbers. *Serves 6 to 8*

GOAT-O GOAT-O SALAD

Make the dressing:
Combine all the dressing ingredients except the oil and salt in a blender or food processor and blend until almost smooth. Slowly drizzle in the oil while still blending. Season to taste with a pinch of salt.

Make the salad:
Make a bed of the lettuce in a large bowl. Arrange the carrots, spring onions, cucumber, peaches, kohlrabi, tomatoes, mint, basil, and peanuts over the lettuce (get creative!) and bring to the table to toss. Serve with enough dressing to coat well.

This salad is on the menu year-round at Girl & the Goat, swapping out various fruits and vegetables depending on the season. In the fall I go for roasted shiitakes and pears. Sometimes in the middle of winter, I do shaved raw butternut squash. But my favorite time of year to make (and eat) this salad is when blueberries are in season. Then I top the whole thing with a dressing inspired by the creamy ginger version you get when you go out for Japanese food, plus some toasted almond slices for crunch. *Serves 6*

KOHLRABI SALAD
WITH GINGER-MAPLE DRESSING

Preheat the oven to 350°F.

Make the dressing:
Combine the mustard, maple syrup, soy sauce, and both vinegars in a blender. Blend just to combine. Add the ginger and shallot, and blend on high for at least 30 seconds, or until a very smooth puree forms. Add the egg yolk and pulse to incorporate. With the blender on medium low, drizzle in the oil to emulsify the dressing. Season to taste with salt.

Make the salad:
Spread the almonds on a sheet tray and toast until golden, about 7 minutes. Set aside to cool.

In a large bowl, toss together the kohlrabi, fennel, lettuce, kale, cheese, and almonds. Drizzle on a good bit of dressing and toss to coat (store any leftover dressing in the fridge for up to 3 days); season to taste with salt and pepper. Add the blueberries and mint, and toss gently. Serve right away.

DRESSING

- 2½ tablespoons Dijon mustard
- 2½ tablespoons maple syrup
- 1½ tablespoons soy sauce
- 1½ tablespoons sherry vinegar
- 1½ tablespoons champagne vinegar
- 2½ tablespoons minced fresh ginger
- 2½ tablespoons minced shallot
- 1 large egg yolk
- 2 cups canola oil
- Salt

SALAD

- ½ cup sliced almonds
- 3 cups peeled and very thinly sliced kohlrabi
- 1 cup thinly sliced fennel bulb
- 3 cups torn Red Oakleaf lettuce
- 2 cups torn lacinato kale leaves (remove stems and ribs before tearing)
- 2 ounces semi-firm salty cheese, such as Evalon goat cheese, MontAmoré cow's-milk cheese, or Parmesan cheese, shaved
- Kosher salt and pepper
- 1 cup fresh blueberries or halved and pitted sweet cherries
- ¼ cup fresh mint leaves, torn

INTERESTING STUFF: KHOLRABI

I know a lot of you out there are scared of kohlrabi because it looks like a weird, alien vegetable. Until I started using it, I had no idea what to do with it. It turns out that it's a German turnip that tastes as if a broccoli stem and a radish had a baby—a little sweet, a little spicy. I recommend using it raw, or just lightly cooking it in a stir-fry, so it still has its crunch.

**GOOD STUFF:
FERMENTED TOFU**

Fermented tofu—*not* to
be confused with stinky
tofu—is one of my favorite
ingredients because it
has a salty funkiness that
I thought I couldn't find
anywhere besides soy
sauce or fish sauce. It's like
nature's MSG, and it adds
this can't-quite-place-it
deliciousness to just about
anything. If you're vegan or
allergic to fish, you can use
it in place of fish sauce in
any of these recipes.

1 cup fresh shiitake
    mushroom caps

¼ cup plus 1 tablespoon
    canola oil

Kosher salt

½ (6-ounce) jar fermented
    tofu in chile (I like the
    Lao Gan Ma brand)

½ cup seasoned rice wine
    vinegar

2 tablespoons toasted
    sesame oil

1 tablespoon yuzu juice

½ tablespoon sambal oelek

1 (24-ounce) package
    soybean noodles,
    dry-packed

2 cups mung bean sprouts

1 cup shredded red cabbage

1 cup thinly sliced baby
    summer squash

½ cup Pickled Fresno Chiles
    (page 263)

¼ cup fresh mint leaves,
    torn

¼ cup fresh Thai basil
    leaves, torn

I buy tofu noodles from Jenny Yang at Phoenix Bean, a tiny tofu kitchen on the north side of Chicago (it's seriously amazing how much tofu she pumps out of that place). She gets her soybeans from local farmers growing them the good old-fashioned way (no GMOs or pesticides), and then makes the most magical, delicious tofu. For these noodles, she cuts extra-firm tofu into thin strips—like linguine, but a little chewier. And they are naturally gluten-free and high in protein! They're great right out of the bag in cold salads or tossed into stir-fries. You can definitely substitute rice noodles, but it's worth trying to find Jenny's—or a similar product—in your area.

For this salad, all you do is toss the noodles with some simple grilled veggies—whatever's at the market—and my very favorite vinaigrette. It's salty, pungent (in a good way), and savory and makes this salad a great one for meat-eaters.

Serves 6

TOFU NOODLE SALAD
WITH FERMENTED TOFU VINAIGRETTE

Preheat the oven to 400°F.

Toss the shiitake mushroom caps with 1 tablespoon of the canola oil and season with a pinch of salt. Spread the mushrooms on a baking sheet and roast until tender, about 8 minutes. Set aside to cool, then slice into quarters.

Combine the fermented tofu, vinegar, remaining ¼ cup canola oil, the sesame oil, yuzu juice, and sambal oelek in a blender and blend until well incorporated and thickened.

Toss the noodles, shiitakes, sprouts, red cabbage, squash, pickled chiles, and herbs with the dressing. Serve at room temperature or chilled.

Giardiniera is an Italian vinegary pickled condiment that goes really well with everything from sandwiches to tacos to eggs, but is mostly known in these parts for topping Italian beef sandwiches. It used to scare me because it's usually really, *really* spicy, and I'm kind of a wuss when it comes to heat. But I love the crunchiness that it adds to a dish, so I wanted to come up with a version that wouldn't melt my face off. I settled on a harissa-vinegar blend that works equally well with carrots (as here), cauliflower in the fall, white asparagus in the spring, and sweet corn or diced golden beets in the summer. *Makes about 1 quart*

BABY CARROT GIARDINIERA

Combine the vegetables, aromatics, and mint in a large heatproof container with a lid.

In a small pot bring the vinegar and ¼ cup water to a boil. Remove from the heat and whisk in the sugar, salt, and harissa until the sugar and salt have dissolved. Pour the hot pickling liquid over the vegetables. Let the mixture come to room temperature, then cover and refrigerate overnight. (This will keep in the refrigerator for up to 1 month.)

2 cups thinly sliced baby carrots

1 large or 2 medium golden beets, diced small (about 1 cup)

1 ear of corn, grilled, kernels cut off the cob

½ cup thinly sliced spring onion bulbs

1 teaspoon thinly sliced jalapeño chile

1 garlic clove, thinly sliced

1 tablespoon torn fresh mint leaves

1 cup distilled white vinegar

½ cup sugar

2 tablespoons salt

1 tablespoon harissa, homemade (page 58) or store-bought

1 pound red beets

¼ cup plus 2 tablespoons extra-virgin olive oil

Kosher salt

1 Hass avocado, halved and pitted

⅓ cup heavy cream

2 tablespoons fresh lemon juice

3 tablespoons sour cream

¼ cup finely chopped Pickled Fresno Chiles (page 263)

½ cup pomelo segments (see page 114), from 1 pomelo

¼ cup diced red onion

¼ cup thinly sliced scallions (white and green parts)

¼ cup perilla leaves, tough ribs removed, leaves chopped

TIP

I am not into fancy methods for roasting perfect beets, such as slathering all this flavor on the outside that won't soak through to the center. I say just toss them lightly with cooking oil and salt, put them in a pan, cover it well with foil, and steam the beets until a paring knife slips right in. If you can smell them cooking, they're done. Just be sure to buy similar-size beets or they won't cook in the same amount of time, and also peel them while they're still warm; the skins will slip right off. I like to do it with paper towels so my hands don't get stained, but you could substitute golden or candy-striped beet varieties if you're not into the mess.

Beets get a bad rap because people think they taste like dirt . . . and I admit that they do have a certain comes-from-the-ground quality. But if you see that earthiness as a positive—and combine the beets with ingredients that balance with their garden-forward flavor—they can be really tasty. A bright pomelo relish does the trick here. Pomelos look just like large, lumpy grapefruits, so I think people assume they taste the same. But when we did a citrus taste test at the restaurant (seriously), we couldn't believe how much sweeter they are than a ruby red grapefruit. Add a little bite from red onions, spice from pickled Fresno chiles, and aromatic freshness from the herbs, and then heap it atop some avocado whipped with sour cream, and you've got a super-refreshing dead-of-winter salad. *Serves 4*

ROASTED BEET SALAD
WITH POMELO RELISH

Preheat the oven to 400°F.

On a large rimmed baking sheet or in a roasting pan, toss the beets with ¼ cup of the oil and season with a generous pinch of salt. Transfer the pan to the oven and roast until the beets are fork-tender, about 45 minutes.

Scoop the flesh out of the avocado. In a small saucepan over low heat, gently simmer the avocado and heavy cream for 15 minutes. Transfer the mixture to a blender and blend until smooth. Add the lemon juice and season with salt. Put in the fridge to chill. Once fully cooled, whisk in the sour cream. Season with more salt, if desired, and keep in the fridge until ready to use.

In a medium bowl, combine the chiles, pomelo, red onion, scallion, perilla leaves, and remaining 2 tablespoons oil. Season with salt.

Remove the beets from the oven, uncover, and let cool slightly. When the beets are just cool enough to handle, peel them; the skins should slide right off. Quarter the beets, then cut the quarters into ¼-inch-thick triangles.

Spread the avocado cream onto a platter. Lay the sliced beets over the crema and sprinkle with the pomelo relish.

Rapini, or broccoli rabe, is a tricky vegetable because it looks like baby broccoli so you think it's going to have that same sweetness. But it's actually pretty bitter. Don't let that stop you, though! This relish will make a convert out of you. Sauté red onions—which are naturally sweet—and toss them with the rapini, plus some salty fish sauce and a little malt vinegar for acid. It's a perfectly balanced situation that is just as tasty heaped onto a sandwich (whether it's crispy chicken or a roast beef sub, especially as a pickle substitute) as it is served with scallops or pork or as a side dish for your Thanksgiving table. *Makes 3 cups*

2 tablespoons canola oil

1 bunch rapini (broccoli rabe), big stems removed, cut into 1-inch pieces

1 small red onion, cut into ¼-inch-thick slices

Salt and pepper

2 tablespoons fish sauce

2 tablespoons malt vinegar

RAPINI RELISH

Heat 1 tablespoon of the oil in a medium sauté pan over high heat. Add half the rapini and stir-fry for 15 seconds. Add half the red onion. Season with salt and pepper and toss. Add 1 tablespoon of the fish sauce and 1 tablespoon of the malt vinegar. Cook about 1 minute longer, or until most of the liquid has cooked down. The rapini should be just tender.

Remove the mixture from the pan and repeat with the remaining ingredients. Serve warm or at room temperature. (Store, covered, in the fridge for up to 2 days.)

4 tablespoons (½ stick) unsalted butter, at room temperature

2 teaspoons cayenne pepper

1 tablespoon canola oil

4 cups corn kernels, freshly cut from the cob

Kosher salt

3 tablespoons fresh lime juice

¼ cup freshly grated Parmesan cheese

2 tablespoons roughly chopped fresh cilantro

When sweet corn is good, it's *good*. You could gnaw on it raw and it'd still be tasty. So when I get a delivery of all that super-fresh, super-sweet goodness, I don't want to do too much to it. This simple dish is inspired by the Mexican street food *elotes*, or corn on the cob that's been smothered with mayo and cheese and cilantro. (I guess technically this version is *esquites*, which just means that the corn's been cut off the cob, but when I changed the name on the menu, people got confused.) Even though I love mayo on everything else in the world, I use cayenne butter here instead (which you should keep in your fridge and slather over baked potatoes), then hit it with a little lime juice, Parm, and cilantro. *Serves 4 to 6*

SWEET CORN ELOTES

In a small bowl, smash together the butter and cayenne.

Heat a large sauté pan over medium-high heat. Add the oil and sauté the corn until just tender, 2 to 3 minutes. Add the cayenne butter and toss to coat. Season with salt and sprinkle in the lime juice and Parmesan. Continue cooking until the butter is fully melted and the corn is tender, about 3 minutes. Sprinkle with the cilantro and serve.

½ cup Dijon mustard

⅓ cup sherry vinegar

⅓ cup white miso paste

1½ tablespoons soy sauce

1½ tablespoons toasted
sesame oil

½ tablespoon sambal oelek

2 cups plus 2 tablespoons
canola oil

2 tablespoons egg yolk

¾ cup freshly grated
Parmesan cheese

1 pound shishito peppers,
rinsed and dried

Salt

¼ cup panko bread crumbs

2 tablespoons toasted
white sesame seeds

When I first opened Girl & the Goat, I wanted to serve jalapeño popper–style stuffed shishito peppers. Shishitos are mostly mild (but sometimes spicy—you never really know), small, long green Japanese peppers that seemed perfect for that treatment. But serving freshly fried shishito poppers turned into a napalm-hot experience. So now I sauté the shishito peppers and then hit them with all the good stuff afterward.

First, there's a miso glaze—made with sesame oil, giving it a nice, rich flavor—and an aioli base to keep things creamy. Then we add Parmesan cheese and pop the whole thing under the broiler so there's a nice crust—sort of an inside-out popper. It's no surprise that this is one of our most popular dishes. *Serves 4 as a side dish*

ROASTED SHISHITO PEPPERS

with SESAME MISO and PARMESAN

Combine the mustard, vinegar, miso paste, soy sauce, sesame oil, and sambal oelek in a blender and blend on low speed just until the ingredients come together. Remove half of the mixture and set aside. Increase the blender speed to medium and drizzle in ½ cup of the canola oil. Transfer the glaze to a bowl.

Combine the reserved mustard mixture and the egg yolk in the blender (no need to clean it first). Blend on medium speed and then slowly drizzle in 1½ cups canola oil. Once the aioli emulsifies, transfer the mixture to a separate bowl and stir in ½ cup of the Parmesan cheese.

Preheat the broiler to high.

Heat the remaining 2 tablespoons canola oil in a large, ovenproof sauté pan over high heat. Add the peppers and season with salt. Toss to coat the peppers and then put them under the broiler until they blister, about 4 minutes. Toss the peppers again and broil them for another 2 to 3 minutes. Remove the peppers from the broiler and drizzle them with the glaze. Toss to coat.

In a small bowl, combine the remaining ¼ cup Parmesan, the bread crumbs, and sesame seeds. Top the peppers with the aioli and the crumb mixture. Put the peppers back under the broiler for 2 to 3 minutes, or until a golden brown crust forms. Serve!

2 tablespoons canola oil

1 head of cauliflower, quartered, any leaves and the core removed, and cut into ¼-inch-thick slices

2 teaspoons kosher salt

3 tablespoons Crunch Butter (recipe follows), at room temperature

½ cup plus 1 tablespoon freshly grated Parmesan cheese

⅓ cup Pickled Hungarian Hots and Bananas (page 262)

2 tablespoons cleaned and julienned preserved lemon peel (recipe follows)

¼ cup plus 1 tablespoon torn fresh mint leaves

¼ cup plus 1 tablespoon toasted pine nuts

When I was little, my mom would make roasted whole cauliflower with cheese sauce. It was the only way I'd eat cauliflower, even though it didn't have much flavor. When I was trying to come up with a new take on a cauliflower dish, I started with something zesty and cheesy (a shout-out to mom): Parmesan. Then I needed something spicy, so in went some pickled peppers. After that, preserved lemon and a little mint for freshness. I wanted it to have some crunch, so I added butter with roasted garlic and panko. Cutting the cauliflower into slices instead of florets helps it cook evenly so that it's perfectly tender all the way through. *Serves 4*

PAN-ROASTED CAULIFLOWER
WITH PICKLED PEPPERS

Heat the oil in a large skillet over high heat. Add the cauliflower and cook, or until caramelized, about 6 minutes. Season with the salt and cook until just tender, 2 to 3 more minutes. Stir in the crunch butter, letting it melt, then toss in ½ cup of the cheese, the pickled peppers, preserved lemon, ¼ cup of the mint, and ¼ cup of the pine nuts. Cook for 2 more minutes. Transfer the cauliflower to a large bowl and garnish with the remaining 1 tablespoon each Parmesan, mint, and pine nuts.

Crunch Butter

Makes 1½ cups

8 tablespoons (1 stick) unsalted butter, at room temperature

2 garlic cloves, minced

5 tablespoons panko bread crumbs

2 tablespoons freshly grated Parmesan cheese

In a small bowl, mash the butter with a fork until softened. Add the garlic, bread crumbs, and Parmesan and mix until fully incorporated. Cover and store in the fridge for up to 1 week.

Preserved Lemons

Makes 1 quart

3 lemons, at room
temperature

½ teaspoon whole pink
peppercorns

½ teaspoon whole fennel seeds

½ teaspoon whole coriander

½ teaspoon mustard seeds

½ cup salt

½ cup sugar

½ cup vodka

Fill a medium stockpot halfway with water and bring to a boil. Using tongs, carefully dunk a 1-quart glass canning jar into the boiling water to sanitize; boil for 10 minutes. Lift out, let drain, and set aside.

Add the lemons to the pot and allow the water to return to a boil. Boil for 5 minutes. Remove the lemons from the water and allow them to cool slightly.

Working on a plate or cutting board with a well to collect the juices, slice one end of each lemon with an X, cutting three-quarters of the way into the fruit. Stack the lemons in the jar so that the uncut end of each lemon sits snuggly inside the cut end of the one below. Add any accumulated juices to the jar as well.

In a small pot over medium-high heat, combine the spices, salt, sugar, and vodka. Cook until the liquid heats all the way through and begins to bubble, about 8 minutes. There will be salt and sugar that have not fully dissolved, so before pouring the mixture into the jar, give it a hard stir. Carefully pour the liquid over the lemons. You may not need all of the liquid but add any remaining solids to the jar. Tightly close the lid and leave the jar at room temperature to preserve for at least 4 weeks or indefinitely.

Store the lemons in the fridge for up to 2 months once opened. To use the preserved lemons, remove a lemon from the jar with clean tongs or a fork. Slice the peel from the flesh and discard the flesh. Clean as much of the white pith off the peel as possible and then slice the peel into thin strips.

**GOOD STUFF:
PRESERVED LEMON**

Preserved lemons, or lemon peels that have been salted, give salty, zingy, citrusy flavor to dishes. I took the traditional Moroccan method and made a few changes to speed things up a bit. First, I boil the lemons, which softens them and helps kick-start the preserving process. Then, I pour a mixture of spices, salt, sugar, and liquor (like vodka) over them. My cooks make fun of me because whenever we talk about a new dish, they can almost bet that it's going to have preserved lemon in it. What can I say? It's that last little touch that helps all the other flavors come to life. Plus, the lemons will last almost forever in your fridge. Just make sure you remove all the white pith (it's super bitter) and slice the peels very thin when using.

1½ cups heavy cream

½ teaspoon crushed red pepper flakes

1 teaspoon light brown sugar

1 teaspoon kosher salt

½ cup blue cheese

3 large sweet potatoes, peeled and sliced into very thin circles

Crispy Onions (recipe follows)

When I was growing up, we always had the classic sweet potato dish with broiled marshmallows on top, but my dad was the only one who liked it. I came up with this sweet-salty-smoky-funky version that's now one of my all-time favorites. It's almost like making a sweet potato lasagna, with thin shavings of sweet potato "noodles" baked between layers of a smoky blue cheese dressing. It's earthy and rich and creamy but still a little sweet—plus then you have salty, crispy onions on top (which are easy to make yourself, but Durkee onions are completely acceptable and delicious).

Serves 4

SWEET POTATO GRATIN
WITH BLUE CHEESE DRESSING
AND CRISPY ONIONS

Preheat the oven to 350°F.

In a small saucepan over low heat, bring the cream to a light simmer. Add the red pepper flakes and brown sugar, and whisk until fully combined. Season with the salt. Crumble the blue cheese into the hot cream and whisk until fully melted and combined.

In a baking dish no larger than 8 inches square, arrange some of the sweet potatoes in a single layer. Cover with ¼ cup of the cream mixture. Repeat until all the ingredients are used, ending with sweet potatoes on the top. Tightly cover the dish with foil and put in the oven to bake until potatoes are fork-tender, 1 hour.

Remove the foil and continue cooking for another 15 minutes. Top with crispy onions and serve.

Crispy Onions

Makes 3 cups

2 cups canola oil

1 small sweet onion, very thinly sliced crosswise and separated into rings

½ cup rice flour

Kosher salt

Heat the oil in a medium saucepan to 275°F.

Toss the onion with the rice flour and shake off any excess. Working in small batches so the oil's temperature doesn't drop, carefully add some of the dredged onion to the oil and fry until golden brown, about 2 minutes. Remove the onions from the oil, transfer to a paper towel–lined plate, and sprinkle with salt. Continue with the remaining onion rings.

1 cup small-diced sweet
onion

1½ tablespoons minced
garlic

2 tablespoons canola oil

Kosher salt

1 tablespoon dry white wine

2 cups medium-diced ripe
tomatoes

½ cup golden raisins

3½ cups maitake mushroom
pieces, any woody stems
removed

3½ cups brown beech
mushrooms, any woody
stems removed

CREMA

1 cup dried shiitake
mushroom caps

1 cup heavy cream

1 cup sour cream

Kosher salt

¼ cup coconut cream

2 teaspoons harissa,
homemade (page 58) or
store-bought

2 teaspoons white miso
paste

1 teaspoon Dijon mustard

1 teaspoon soy sauce

1½ tablespoons brine-
packed small capers

Kosher salt

This is the vegetable answer to a Bolognese sauce. It gets deep, meaty flavor from wild mushrooms, saltiness from the miso and capers, tang from the tomatoes, and sweetness from the golden raisins. I finish it with a little rich coconut cream and a drizzle of mushroom-infused crema. Is it vegan and gluten-free? Absolutely. Does it taste like it? Absolutely not. You could serve this over pasta or roasted squash, or even eat it on its own. *Serves 4 to 6*

MUSHROOM RAGOUT

Make the ragout:
In a medium saucepan over medium heat, cook the onion and garlic in the oil with a pinch of salt until translucent and soft, about 3 minutes. Deglaze the pan with the white wine, using your spoon to scrape up any bits stuck to the bottom of the pan. Add the tomatoes and raisins, and let the mixture simmer until the tomatoes break down and the raisins are half-rehydrated, 20 minutes.

Add the maitake mushrooms and season with a pinch of salt. Make sure that this first batch of mushrooms has thoroughly wilted, about 5 minutes, before adding the beech mushrooms. When all the mushrooms have been added, simmer over medium heat until the mushrooms are soft, the tomatoes are broken down, and the raisins are rehydrated, about 1 hour.

Meanwhile, make the crema:
In a medium sauté pan over medium heat, simmer the mushroom caps in the heavy cream for 15 minutes to rehydrate. Strain the cream into a medium bowl, discarding the mushrooms. Let cool, and then fold in the sour cream. Season to taste with salt.

To finish the ragout, stir in the coconut cream, harissa, miso paste, mustard, soy sauce, and capers; continue to simmer gently for 15 minutes. The sauce should be thin enough to coat noodles or vegetables; do not over-reduce. Season to taste with salt.

Serve the mushroom ragout topped with the crema.

FARMERS' MARKET
Picnic

. . . .

Whether it's for an afternoon trip to the beach, an outdoor concert, or a movie at the park, picnicking is all about packing up a bunch of simple things that you can pile onto crusty bread or that everyone can snack on while they're busy doing something else. It's also the perfect time to showcase whatever market finds you got that week.

I love using the farmers' market as my inspiration because there's always a surprise! You never know what treasures you're going to find, plus there's the countdown to seeing your favorites appear as they come into season. I sometimes hear that people get overwhelmed browsing the market for ingredients because they don't always know what to do with their purchases. But that's what the farmers are there for! They love answering questions about their products, and they always have great ideas for how to cook them. These recipes are a great starting point, especially because you can swap in lots of other fruits, veggies, and fresh herbs.

1 pound fresh strawberries

1 pound vine-ripened tomatoes, quartered

1 red bell pepper, cored and seeded

1 shallot, roughly chopped

1 (8- to 10-inch) cucumber, peeled and roughly chopped

1 fresh Thai chile, or to taste

¼ cup tomato paste

¼ cup olive oil

2 tablespoons salt, plus more as needed

This play on the traditional chilled tomato soup gets just the right amount of sweetness from fresh summer berries. I also throw in a little bit of Thai chile for a hint of heat. Then I top it off with sliced avocado for some richness, which also balances the acidity of the fruit. *Serves 6*

STRAWBERRY GAZPACHO

Combine all the ingredients in a blender, and process until almost smooth; it should still have a little texture. Season to taste with additional salt as needed. Serve at room temperature or slightly chilled.

While Americans are used to salads made primarily of lettuce with a bunch of things thrown in them, Moroccan salads are usually a vegetable that has been stewed with all kinds of spices until it falls apart, and is then served at room temperature. Zaalouk is an eggplant-and-tomato version of this idea, which gets its complex flavor from ingredients such as preserved lemon, harissa, and olives.

Serves 6 as an appetizer

EGGPLANT ZAALOUK

Heat a large, preferably nonstick pan over medium-high heat. Add 1 tablespoon of the oil and sauté the eggplant, stirring regularly, until browned and soft, about 10 minutes. You may need to add a small amount of oil while cooking if the pan gets completely dry.

In a large heavy-bottomed pot, heat the remaining 1 tablespoon oil over medium heat and then sweat the onion and garlic until aromatic and soft, about 5 minutes. Add the diced tomatoes and simmer until some of the liquid has evaporated, about 20 minutes.

Deglaze the pan with the wine, then add the eggplant, and cook for 15 more minutes. Stir in the harissa and preserved lemon, season with a pinch of salt, reduce the heat to medium low, and cook for 30 minutes.

Remove the pot from the heat and stir in the mint and olives. Season to taste with salt. Let cool to room temperature before serving. (This can be stored in the refrigerator for up to 5 days.)

2 tablespoons canola oil, or more if needed

2 pounds Japanese eggplant, sliced lengthwise in half and then into ½-inch-thick half-moons

1 medium sweet onion, diced

5 garlic cloves, minced

4 large ripe heirloom tomatoes, diced

¼ cup dry white wine

1½ tablespoons harissa, homemade (page 58) or store-bought

¼ cup julienned preserved lemon peel (½ lemon before cutting; page 198)

Kosher salt

2 tablespoons chopped fresh mint

¼ cup large green olives, pitted and sliced lengthwise

1 pound fresh sweet cherries, pitted and halved

½ cup packed torn fresh basil leaves

¼ cup Pickled Fresno Chiles (page 263)

3 tablespoons extra-virgin olive oil

1 tablespoon fish sauce

1 tablespoon champagne vinegar

1 pound cream cheese, at room temperature

½ pound drained feta cheese, crumbled

½ cup heavy cream

¼ teaspoon kosher salt

Cherries have always been a tricky thing for me; I don't like them cooked because they taste like cherry pie filling. When I pickle them, they get a little too tart, and if you try pitting and slicing them too far ahead of serving, they start to turn brown. But, I found that if you toss them with a little vinegar and fish sauce, they stay bright and sweet, and just a little tart. Balanced with some fresh basil and pickled chiles, they are great over whipped feta, as well as pork chops, chicken, or pretty much anything off the grill. *Makes 3 cups*

MARINATED SWEET CHERRIES
WITH WHIPPED FETA

In a large bowl, mix the cherries, basil, chiles, oil, fish sauce, and vinegar.

In stand mixer with the paddle attachment or in a large bowl with a hand mixer or wooden spoon, beat the cream cheese until fluffy, about 2 minutes. Add the crumbled feta, cream, and salt and mix for another minute.

Serve the cherries spooned over the whipped feta.

Instead of dicing cooked chicken breast for a salad, I like to brine a whole chicken, roast it, then pick the meat off the bones—tasty skin bits and all. You end up with tons more flavor. To add another level of yum, I fold in green goddess dressing, an old-school ranchlike classic that's freshened up with scallions and tarragon. *Serves 8*

GREEN GODDESS CHICKEN SALAD

Make the chicken:

In a very large pot over medium heat, combine the onion, salt, sugar, garlic, peppercorns, coriander, red pepper flakes, and 4 cups water. Bring the mixture to a boil and whisk until the sugar and salt are fully dissolved. Add the orange and thyme. Remove from the heat and let cool for 15 minutes. Add the ice cubes to the brine, allow to cool to room temperature, then submerge the chickens. Refrigerate for 8 hours.
Preheat the oven to 425°F.

Transfer the chickens to a roasting pan. Discard the brine. Roast the chickens for 30 minutes. Reduce the oven temperature to 375°F and continue roasting for 1 hour more. The chickens' juices will run clear when the meat is fully cooked. Remove the chickens from the oven and allow them to rest for 20 minutes. Remove the skin and chop into pieces. Shred the meat into medium pieces. Refrigerate until ready to use.

Make the dressing:

In a food processor or blender, combine the egg yolks, lemon juice, lime juice, and mustard. Blend until fully combined. While the food processor is running, slowly drizzle in the oil and continue mixing until the dressing thickens. Add the sour cream, scallions, and chopped tarragon. Blend until well combined.

Heat the 1 tablespoon oil in a medium sauté pan over medium-high heat. Cook the onions until tender, about 5 minutes. Transfer to a large bowl and let cool.

Add the chicken, chopped skin, dressing, and the basil and tarragon leaves to the onions. Season with salt to taste and toss to coat. (If you plan on doing the preparation ahead, the chicken can be stored in the refrigerator, undressed, for up to 4 days. Dress the salad right before serving.)

CHICKEN

1 medium white onion, quartered

1 cup kosher salt

¾ cup sugar

2 tablespoons roughly chopped garlic

1 tablespoon black peppercorns

1 teaspoon ground coriander

¼ teaspoon crushed red pepper flakes

1 orange, quartered

1 tablespoon fresh thyme leaves

4 cups ice cubes

2 (3- to 4-pound) whole chickens

DRESSING

2 egg yolks

3 tablespoons fresh lemon juice

3 tablespoons fresh lime juice

1½ tablespoons Dijon mustard

1 cup canola oil

⅔ cup sour cream

1 cup chopped scallions (white and green parts)

⅓ cup chopped fresh tarragon

1 tablespoon canola oil

2 cups thinly sliced sweet onions

¼ cup torn fresh basil leaves

2 tablespoons torn fresh tarragon leaves

Kosher salt

KEEPING IT SWEET

ALMOND PANNA COTTA
with Soy Drizzle and
Almond-Sesame Brittle.............. *217*

GOAT CHEESECAKE
with Beer Caramel and
Pretzel Whipped Cream *220*

APPLE FRITTERS
with Cider Glaze *224*

**SWEET CORN
FROZEN NOUGAT**
with Tart Plums and Basil.............. *227*

**STICKY SWEET
POTATO CAKE**
with Blueberry-Tomatillo Jam *229*

**PEANUT BUTTER
OVERLOAD CAKE**
with Concord Grape Sauce *231*

OLIVE OIL CAKE
with Strawberries and Limoncello *235*

CHOCOLATE MOUSSE
with Black Olive Caramel *236*

MANGO PARFAIT
with Coconut Cloud.................. *239*

**PASSIONFRUIT
MERINGUE PIE** *243*

**BLUEBERRY-STRAWBERRY
HAND PIES** *244*

Ice Cream for Dinner

ICE CREAMS

Basic Recipe *248*

Mint Chocolate Chip *248*

Blueberry Swirl *248*

Salted Peanut *248*

Fennel-Orange *249*

Cajeta *249*

TOPPINGS

Mom's Chocolate
Fudge Sauce *249*

Chocolate Crunch *250*

Inside-Out Malt Balls *250*

Brown Sugar-Cayenne
Caramel *250*

Caramel Popcorn Crunch *251*

Toasted Marshmallow Creme *251*

COOKIES

Chocolate Chunk *252*

Oatmeal-Cranberry *252*

Peanut Butter
Sandwich *253*

Wookie Pies *254*

ONE THING I REMEMBER MOST FROM WHEN I WAS YOUNG WAS THAT my dad was *obsessed* with dessert. If there wasn't any dessert in the house, he'd have a tantrum. One time my friend Sue ate his last mini cherry pie, and I've never seen his face get so red. I still believe that a meal should always end with something sweet—but not *too* sweet. My favorite dessert dishes are ones that mash up all different flavor profiles—tangy, salty, bitter, sweet—just like when I'm cooking something savory.

PANNA COTTA

1½ cups sliced almonds

2¾ cups whole milk

1 tablespoon unflavored
powdered gelatin

2 cups heavy cream

¾ cup sugar

½ teaspoon kosher salt

SOY DRIZZLE

¾ cup balsamic vinegar

3 tablespoons sugar

1 tablespoon sweet soy
sauce

Almond-Sesame Brittle
(recipe follows)

Spiced Krispies (recipe
follows)

Sesame Whip (recipe
follows)

When Gary and I were visiting Taiwan, we kept seeing vendors selling little containers of what we were told was "almond tofu." We didn't think it sounded particularly appealing, but surprisingly it reminded me of a panna cotta, which is traditionally sweetened cream that's been thickened with gelatin. I took that idea and ran with it, adding a balsamic vinegar–soy sauce syrup for some brightness, along with a few other goodies like Almond-Sesame Brittle and Spiced Krispies. But if you're pressed for time, you can leave out the brittle. *Serves 8*

ALMOND PANNA COTTA
WITH SOY DRIZZLE
AND ALMOND-SESAME BRITTLE

Preheat the oven to 325°F.

Make the panna cotta:
Spread the almonds on a sheet tray. Toast in the oven to a golden caramel brown, 5 to 10 minutes, tossing once or twice to ensure even toasting.

While the almonds toast, pour ¾ cup of the milk into a bowl and sprinkle the gelatin over the top. Combine the remaining 2 cups milk, the cream, sugar, salt, and 3 tablespoons water in a medium saucepan over medium heat. Add the almonds directly from the oven to the pan. Simmer for 5 minutes. Remove from the heat and allow to infuse for 5 minutes.

Transfer the mixture to a blender and buzz on high until a smooth thick liquid forms. Strain through a fine-mesh sieve into a bowl. Stir in the gelatin mixture. Portion evenly into ramekins or individual bowls and refrigerate until set, at least 3 hours or overnight.

Make the soy drizzle:
In a small saucepan, combine all the ingredients. Bring to a boil and reduce the heat so that the liquid simmers. Cook until reduced by half, about 15 minutes. The sauce should be the thickness of maple syrup. Allow to cool before using.

(Continues)

To serve the dessert, poke a hole in the center of each panna cotta and fill with soy drizzle, about 1 teaspoon per dish. Top with a handful of crumbled brittle, followed with some krispies. Finish each with a dollop of sesame whip.

Almond-Sesame Brittle

This is inspired by the enormous blocks of peanut brittle you see Taipei street vendors shaving down for *hua sheng bing*—basically, ice cream burritos. Crumble it to top panna cotta, ice cream, cereal—you name it.

Makes 2 cups

Butter

2 cups sugar

1 cup sliced almonds, toasted

3 tablespoons sesame seeds, toasted

Grease a spatula and rimmed baking sheet with butter.

Combine the sugar and ½ cup water in a medium saucepan. Heat over medium heat without stirring until caramelized. The sugar will begin to melt and turn golden brown after about 15 minutes. Turn off the heat and carefully add the almonds and sesame seeds. Quickly stir with the buttered spatula and pour onto the prepared baking sheet. Spread until ¼ inch thick and then allow to set, about 30 minutes. Break into small pieces. These can be stored in a container at room temperature for up to 2 days.

Spiced Krispies

Crispy rice cereal browned in butter and sprinkled with spice—need I say more?

Makes 1 cup

2 tablespoons unsalted butter

1 cup crispy rice cereal

1 teaspoon garam masala

In a medium skillet, heat the butter over medium heat until melted. Add the rice cereal and garam masala and toss to coat. Cook until the cereal is lightly toasted and fragrant, about 5 minutes. Remove from the heat. This can be stored in a container at room temperature for up to 2 days.

Sesame Whip

Save some for your coffee!

Makes 2¼ cups

2 cups heavy cream

¼ cup sweetened condensed milk

1 teaspoon toasted sesame oil

In a stand mixer fitted with the whisk attachment or in a large bowl with a hand mixer or whisk, whip the cream, condensed milk, and sesame oil until soft peaks form. Use the whipped cream immediately or cover and store the unwhipped mixture in the fridge for up to 5 days.

Every year for my dad's birthday we would come up with a different cheesecake creation for him, playing around with different styles and toppings. I think this version beats them all. I make the cake with tangy goat cheese, so it's light and fluffy and has just the right amount of richness. Then I top it with Beer Caramel, which is malty and slightly bitter, and Pretzel Whipped Cream—both are the amazing discoveries of one of our pastry cooks, Hannah. And both would also be awesome additions to Ice Cream for Dinner (page 247). *Makes 1 (10-inch) cake*

GOAT CHEESECAKE
with BEER CARAMEL
and PRETZEL WHIPPED CREAM

Preheat the oven to 350°F. Wrap a 10-inch springform pan tightly with foil and spray the bottom with nonstick cooking spray.

In a food processor, pulse together the pretzels, Cheez-Its, and white chocolate chips until ground to fine crumbs, being careful not to melt the chocolate. Drizzle the melted butter over the crumbs and pulse two or three more times, until the ingredients just come together.

Press the pretzel crust into an even layer on the bottom of the pan. Bake until toasted and firm, 10 minutes, and then cool completely.

Reduce the oven temperature to 300°F.

In a large pot, bring 3 quarts of water to a boil.

In the bowl of a stand mixer fitted with the paddle attachment, combine the cream cheese and goat cheese, and beat until completely smooth, scraping the bowl several times. Add the sour cream and mix until smooth. Add the sugar, salt, and vanilla bean seeds. Mix until combined, scraping the bowl again, and with the mixer on low speed, slowly pour in half the beaten eggs. Mix to incorporate, scrape the sides again, and slowly add the remaining beaten eggs. Mix until smooth, scraping the bowl one last time.

Nonstick cooking spray

1 cup broken pretzels, plus more for garnish

1½ cups broken pieces of Cheez-Its

⅓ cup white chocolate chips

2 tablespoons unsalted butter, melted

1 pound cream cheese, at room temperature

1 pound fresh goat cheese, at room temperature

2½ cups sour cream

2 cups sugar

2½ teaspoons kosher salt

2 vanilla beans, split in half lengthwise and seeds scraped

5 large eggs, beaten

Pretzel Whipped Cream (recipe follows)

Beer Caramel (recipe follows)

(Continues)

Pour the cheesecake filling into the baked crust and put the springform pan in a roasting pan. Transfer both to the oven and then carefully pour enough of the boiling water into the roasting pan to come about halfway up the sides of the cheesecake pan. Bake for 60 to 75 minutes, until the edges of the cheesecake are set but the middle is still slightly jiggly.

Carefully remove the springform pan from the oven (leave the roasting pan in the oven for now and come back for it later). Let the cheesecake cool completely on a wire rack. Refrigerate, uncovered, until ready to serve—at least an hour or up to 3 days.

To serve, release the cake from the pan and carefully transfer it to a serving platter. Top with most of the whipped cream and drizzle with about half of the caramel. Add additional whipped cream, caramel, and pretzel pieces to individual slices as desired.

Pretzel Whipped Cream

Makes 4 cups

1½ cups heavy cream   1 tablespoon sugar
½ cup broken pretzels

In a small saucepan over medium-low heat, bring the cream, pretzels, and sugar to a simmer. Remove the pot from the heat. Cover the pot with a lid and let the mixture steep for 30 minutes so the flavors can infuse. Strain the mixture, discarding the solids, and chill the cream completely, at least 1 hour or overnight.

In a stand mixer fitted with the whisk attachment or in a large bowl with a hand mixer or whisk, whip the cream mixture until soft peaks form. Use immediately or cover and store in the fridge for up to 5 days.

Beer Caramel

Makes 2 cups

6 ounces hoppy beer of choice

Zest of ½ grapefruit, cut into long strips

1 tablespoon unsalted butter

¾ cup dark brown sugar

½ cup heavy cream

½ teaspoon vanilla extract

Generous pinch of salt

In a small saucepan over medium heat, bring the beer and grapefruit zest to a simmer and cook until reduced to about 1 cup, 10 minutes.

Remove the zest and add the butter and brown sugar. Bring the mixture to a boil and cook until it reduces to the consistency of thick maple syrup, 10 minutes. Add the cream, vanilla extract, and salt, and continue cooking until thickened, about 15 more minutes.

Let the caramel cool completely. Serve at room temperature or slightly warmed. It will last in the fridge in a covered container for up to 5 days.

Our pastry chef Nick's version of an apple fritter is like an awesome doughnut with tasty chunks of apple and a salty-sweet glaze made with apple cider, soy sauce, and balsamic vinegar. These are just as good after they've sat out for a bit as when they emerge fresh out of the fryer. They make the perfect simple fall dessert—especially with MontAmoré Ice Cream (page 230)! *Makes 8 fritters*

APPLE FRITTERS
WITH CIDER GLAZE

Make the fritters:
In a sauté pan over medium heat, combine the apples, brown sugar, cornstarch, ½ teaspoon cinnamon, and ½ teaspoon salt. Cook until the mixture has thickened, 5 minutes.

In the bowl of a stand mixer fitted with the dough hook, combine the flour, granulated sugar, butter, egg yolk, milk, yeast, vanilla, remaining 1 tablespoon salt, and ¾ cup of water. Mix on medium speed until a dough balls forms, then fold in the apple mixture.

Transfer the dough to a large bowl and cover. Let dough double in size at room temperature, about 30 minutes.

Spray a baking sheet with nonstick cooking spray and line with parchment paper.

Holding the dough, gently knead in the remaining 1 tablespoon cinnamon using your hands. On a lightly floured work surface, roll out the dough to a large piece ½ inch thick. Cut into 8 pieces. Put the dough onto the prepared baking sheet and let it rise again at room temperature for 15 minutes. Transfer to the fridge to chill for at least 3 hours or overnight.

Make the glaze:
Mix the confectioners' sugar, apple cider, soy sauce, and vinegar until slightly thick.

In a large pot, heat the canola oil to 350°F. Line a plate with paper towels.

Working in batches and making sure not to overcrowd, fry the fritters, turning once, until they are a caramel color, about 3 minutes, and then transfer to the prepared plate to drain. Drizzle the fritters with the glaze and serve warm.

FRITTERS

3 tart apples, such as Fuji or Honeycrisp, peeled, cored, and diced small

¼ cup light brown sugar

½ tablespoon cornstarch

1 tablespoon plus ½ teaspoon ground cinnamon

1 tablespoon plus ½ teaspoon kosher salt

4 cups all-purpose flour, plus more for rolling

⅓ cup granulated sugar

4 tablespoons (½ stick) unsalted butter, at room temperature

1 large egg yolk

3 tablespoons evaporated or whole milk

1 tablespoon active dry yeast

½ tablespoon vanilla extract

Nonstick cooking spray

CIDER GLAZE

1 cup confectioners' sugar

2 tablespoons apple cider

½ teaspoon soy sauce

¼ teaspoon balsamic vinegar

2 quarts canola oil, for frying

Kernels from 2 ears of corn

⅔ cup heavy cream

1½ teaspoons kosher salt

2 cups sugar

8 large egg whites

2 tart plums, pitted and
sliced thin, for serving

Torn fresh basil, for serving

Frozen nougat is a fun way to make a great creamy ice cream–like dessert without an ice cream machine. The combination of Italian meringue and whipped cream freezes to a smooth, rich texture. I wanted to make a version with sweet corn because when corn is in season, it tastes just like candy. The nougat sets in a shallow glass dish and then is served layered with tart plums and fresh basil or mint.

Makes 2 quarts

SWEET CORN FROZEN NOUGAT
WITH TART PLUMS AND BASIL

In a medium saucepan over medium heat, heat the corn kernels until just soft. Add the cream and salt, and bring to a low simmer for about 5 minutes. Transfer to a bowl that is resting in another bowl filled with ice cubes. Cool completely.

Transfer to a blender and puree until smooth. Strain through a fine-mesh strainer into a large bowl.

Bring a medium pot of water to a simmer. Heat the sugar and egg whites in a heatproof bowl set over the simmering water until the sugar is completely dissolved and the mixture is hot to the touch, 5 minutes. Strain egg white mixture through a fine-mesh sieve (to remove any cooked bits of egg white) into a small stand mixer bowl fitted with a whisk attachment. Whip the egg white mixture on high until doubled in volume. Let cool to room temperature.

Add one-third of the meringue to the cooled and strained corn base and stir with a whisk until completely combined. Add the next third of the meringue and fold in using a rubber spatula until almost completely combined. Add remaining meringue and fold until all of the meringue is incorporated.

Line a 5½ by 3-inch loaf pan with parchment paper. Pour the corn nougat into the pan and freeze for at least 3 hours and up to 2 weeks. Serve scoops of nougat topped with plum slices and basil.

CAKE

Nonstick cooking spray or butter

1 pound sweet potatoes

1 cup all-purpose flour

2 teaspoons baking powder

1 teaspoon baking soda

1 teaspoon kosher salt

½ teaspoon ground cinnamon

½ teaspoon ground ginger

4 tablespoons (½ stick) unsalted butter, at room temperature

½ cup granulated sugar

2 large eggs, at room temperature

1 teaspoon vanilla extract

BROWN SUGAR CARAMEL

8 tablespoons (1 stick) unsalted butter

1 cup dark brown sugar

¾ cup heavy cream

½ teaspoon kosher salt

Blueberry-Tomatillo Jam (page 47)

MontAmoré Ice Cream (recipe follows)

This is my twist on the more traditional—and equally as tasty—sticky date cake. It's so moist and delicious that you may find yourself making this batter into sweet potato muffins for brunch or sweet potato cupcakes with a simple icing. But for dessert, I like to bake it as a cake and warm it with a simple toffee sauce to make it sticky and rich. It pairs perfectly with a salty-sweet cheese ice cream and tangy blueberry-tomatillo jam. It's like the perfect cheese plate turned into a dessert! Substitute store-bought sour cream or goat cheese ice cream if you'd like, or even a store-bought blueberry jam. *Makes 1 (9-inch) cake*

STICKY SWEET POTATO CAKE
WITH BLUEBERRY-TOMATILLO JAM

Make the cake:

Preheat the oven to 350°F. Prepare a 9-inch cake pan by spraying with nonstick spray or greasing with butter. Line the bottom with a circle of parchment paper.

Roast the sweet potatoes until extremely soft when pierced with a knife, 45 minutes to 1 hour. Halve the potatoes, scoop out the flesh, and transfer to a food processor (discard the skin). Puree until very smooth.

In a medium bowl, combine the flour, baking powder, baking soda, salt, cinnamon, and ginger.

In the bowl of a stand mixer fitted with the paddle attachment, beat the butter and granulated sugar until well combined. Mix in the eggs and vanilla and then scrape the sides of the bowl. Add the sweet potato puree and mix until well combined. Add the flour mixture and mix until just incorporated.

Transfer the batter to the prepared pan and bake until a toothpick inserted in the center comes out clean, 25 minutes. Cool the cake in the pan until just room temperature and then gently remove.

(Continues)

Make the caramel:

Melt the butter in a small saucepan over medium heat. Add the brown sugar and allow to warm for 5 minutes. Whisk in the cream. Simmer until the sugar dissolves and is no longer grainy, about 10 minutes. Whisk in the salt. Remove from the heat. Once cool, this can be stored in the refrigerator for up to 5 days. Rewarm the sauce before serving.

To serve, drizzle slices of the cake with the caramel and top with the jam. Serve with a scoop of ice cream.

MontAmoré Ice Cream

Makes 1 quart

1 pint half-and-half

½ cup sugar

2 large eggs

⅓ cup MontAmoré cheese, finely grated (see note, page 33)

½ teaspoon fresh lemon juice

¼ teaspoon kosher salt

In a medium saucepan over medium heat, warm the half-and-half and sugar until just under a boil, about 5 minutes.

In a small bowl, whisk together the eggs. Whisk ¼ cup of the hot cream mixture into the eggs and then transfer back to the sauce-pan. Reduce the heat to medium low. Using a wooden spoon, stir the mixture until it thickens and coats the back of spoon, about 8 minutes. Stir in the cheese, lemon juice, and salt. Allow the cheese to melt fully, then pour the mixture into a bowl that's rest-ing over a bowl of ice cubes and let cool completely.

Transfer the mixture to a blender and process. Pass through a fine-mesh sieve into a covered container. Refrigerate overnight.

Follow the instructions for your ice cream maker to churn the ice cream. Freeze for at least 3 hours before serving.

CAKE

Nonstick cooking spray

2½ cups all-purpose flour

2 teaspoons baking soda

1½ teaspoons baking powder

1 cup (2 sticks) unsalted butter, at room temperature

1½ cups sugar

1 cup creamy peanut butter

3 large eggs

2 cups buttermilk

BRITTLE

⅔ cup creamy peanut butter

½ cup sugar

½ cup light corn syrup

1 tablespoon unsalted butter

1½ teaspoons baking soda

1 teaspoon vanilla extract

MERINGUE

3 large egg whites

⅓ cup sugar

Pinch of cream of tartar

⅓ cup creamy peanut butter

GRAPE SYRUP

2 cups Concord grape juice

¾ cup sugar

⅓ teaspoon citric acid, or 2 teaspoons lemon juice

This dessert is for anyone who grew up loving peanut-butter-and-jelly sandwiches (and probably still does). It was inspired by my search for new ways to add some crunch to our pastry menu. I came across this peanut butter brittle recipe, which doesn't make the usual stick-to-your-molars, toffee-like brittle. Instead, the fat from the peanut butter keeps it creamier, like the flaky inside of a Butterfinger. After discovering that, I knew I had to make a dessert to showcase all that peanut buttery goodness. This cake is perfectly moist with just enough peanut flavor. I top it with fluffy peanut butter, sprinkle that peanut butter brittle on top, add a scoop of Salted Peanut Ice Cream (page 248), and drizzle it all with tart Concord grape syrup. *Makes 1 (9 by 13-inch) cake*

PEANUT BUTTER OVERLOAD CAKE
WITH CONCORD GRAPE SAUCE

Make the cake:

Preheat the oven to 350°F. Grease a 9 by 13-inch baking pan with cooking spray and line with parchment paper.

In a large bowl, whisk together the flour, baking soda, and baking powder. In the bowl of a stand mixer fitted with the paddle attachment, beat together the butter, sugar, and peanut butter on high speed until light and fluffy. Scrape the sides and bottom of the bowl. Reduce the speed to medium and add the eggs, one at a time, until fully incorporated. Reduce the speed to low and add about a third of the flour mixture, followed by 1 cup of the buttermilk. Continue alternating adding the flour mixture and buttermilk, ending with the flour, mixing until everything is just incorporated.

Scrape the batter into the prepared pan and bake until a toothpick inserted in the center comes out clean, 35 to 40 minutes. Put the pan on a wire rack to cool for 10 minutes, then remove the cake from the pan, and let it cool completely.

Line 2 large baking sheets with parchment paper.

(Continues)

Make the brittle:

Warm the peanut butter in a double boiler or microwave until just melted. In a small, nonreactive saucepan over medium-high heat, combine the sugar, corn syrup, butter, and 3½ teaspoons water and cook until the mixture reaches 295°F. Remove the pan from the heat and stir in the baking soda; be careful as the mixture will bubble up. Carefully stir in the vanilla, then whisk in the melted peanut butter until smooth. Pour the mixture onto the prepared trays and let cool completely at room temperature.

Break the brittle into large chunks and pulse in a food processor into small shards. (Store in an airtight container for up to 3 days.)

Make the meringue:

In a double boiler or a medium stainless-steel bowl set on top of a small pot of barely simmering water, whisk together the egg whites, sugar, and cream of tartar. Cook until the sugar has dissolved and the whites are warmed, about 6 minutes. Transfer to the bowl of a stand mixer fitted with the whisk attachment, and whip the egg white mixture on high speed until stiff peaks form and the meringue is glossy, about 5 minutes. Transfer one-third of the meringue to a small bowl and fold in the peanut butter. Then carefully fold the mixture into the remaining meringue.

Make the syrup:

In a small saucepan over medium heat, bring the grape juice, sugar, and citric acid to a simmer. Cook until the mixture is slightly thickened, about the consistency of honey, 30 minutes. Strain the sauce through a fine-mesh strainer into a small bowl and let cool completely.

To serve, top slices of the cake with meringue and use a kitchen torch to caramelize the top. Sprinkle with the brittle and drizzle with some of the grape syrup.

Nonstick cooking spray

1 pound fresh strawberries, hulled and quartered

1 cup limoncello liqueur

1 cup high-quality olive oil

4 large eggs

2¼ cups sugar

½ vanilla bean, split lengthwise and seeds scraped

1 teaspoon grated orange zest

¼ cup buttermilk

2⅓ cups all-purpose flour

1⅛ teaspoons baking powder

1¼ teaspoons kosher salt

A few years ago I visited an olive grove in California where I got to taste olive oils side by side. They had all been pressed at the same farm, just over a period of time. The variation in flavor from just one week to the next was incredible—some were bright and fruity, others earthy and herbaceous. This cake is all about showcasing a great, high-quality olive oil that's a little spicy and not too grassy. Keeping the Italian theme (because nothing is more Italian than olive oil), it pairs beautifully with strawberries macerated in limoncello (cherries would be awesome, too) and sugar-coated shaved lemon peel. *Makes 1 (11 by 15-inch or 9 by 5-inch) cake*

OLIVE OIL CAKE
WITH STRAWBERRIES AND LIMONCELLO

Preheat the oven to 325°F. Grease an 11 by 15-inch jelly roll pan or a 9 by 5-inch loaf pan with cooking spray and line with parchment paper.

In a large bowl, toss together the strawberries and limoncello, and let macerate for about 20 minutes.

Reserve 2 tablespoons of the olive oil to brush on the cake. In a large bowl, mix the remaining olive oil, the eggs, sugar, vanilla seeds, and orange zest. Whisking by hand or using a hand mixer on low speed, add the buttermilk in a steady stream and mix until completely incorporated. Sift the flour, baking powder, and salt over the egg mixture and gently fold in until just combined.

Pour the batter into the prepared pan. Bake, rotating the pan halfway through, until the middle is completely baked through, 20 to 25 minutes. The cake's edges might get a little dark, but don't worry; you can trim them off for serving.

Brush the cake with the reserved olive oil while still hot. Let the cake cool completely in the pan, then cut into 2 by 2-inch pieces (if using the jelly roll pan) or 1-inch slices (if using the loaf pan). Serve with the macerated strawberries and limoncello on the side.

I first made this caramel back when I owned Scylla, and it was intended to pair with a seared tuna dish. I worked the pastry station quite a bit coming up as a cook, so I've always liked to use pastry techniques in my savory dishes. I figured that adding the olives would make a briny twist on salted caramel. I still love this sauce, but these days I'm more excited about pairing that salty savoriness with a simple chocolate mousse to make a new, totally unexpected combo. *Serves 8*

CHOCOLATE MOUSSE

WITH BLACK OLIVE CARAMEL

Make the mousse:

In a stand mixer fitted with the whisk attachment or in a large bowl with a whisk, whip 2⅔ cups of the cream until soft peaks form. Store in the fridge until ready to use.

In a medium saucepan over medium heat, combine the milk, the remaining 1⅓ cups cream, the vanilla seeds, ½ teaspoon of the salt, and ¼ cup of the sugar. Allow the mixture to start bubbling rapidly around the edges but not reach a full boil. Turn off the heat.

In a double boiler or a heatproof glass or metal bowl set on top of a small pot of barely simmering water, whisk together the egg yolks and remaining ¼ cup sugar. Cook, whisking constantly, until warmed through and thickened, about 6 minutes.

Whisk about half of the warmed vanilla bean and milk mixture into the yolk mixture, then add the yolk mixture to the remaining milk mixture in the saucepan. Continue cooking and whisking over low heat until thickened slightly, 6 to 8 minutes.

Pour the custard through a fine-mesh strainer into a medium heatproof bowl with the chocolate and remaining 1½ teaspoons salt. Set the bowl over a small pot of barely simmering water. Cook, stirring, until all the chocolate has melted, about 5 minutes. (Alternatively, combine them in a medium bowl and heat in the microwave in 10-second pulses.)

(Continues)

CHOCOLATE MOUSSE

1 quart heavy cream

1 cup whole milk

½ vanilla bean, split lengthwise and seeds scraped

2 teaspoons kosher salt

½ cup sugar

5 egg yolks

2½ cups semi-sweet chocolate chips

Chocolate Crunch (page 250)

BLACK OLIVE CARAMEL

1⅓ cups sugar

⅓ cup strained fresh orange juice

⅓ cup heavy cream

½ cup pitted and chopped Niçoise olives

¼ teaspoon kosher salt

Remove the custard-chocolate mixture from the heat and let it cool to room temperature. Whisk in 1 cup of the whipped cream. Carefully fold in another 3 cups of the whipped cream to finish off the mousse. Reserve the remaining whipped cream for serving; cover and return to the fridge.

Line the bottom of an 8-inch springform pan with the chocolate crunch pieces. Smash them down with a spoon. Spoon the mousse over the top of the crunch. Put in the freezer for at least 2 hours to set. (The mousse can be stored in the refrigerator for up to 1 week, but is firmer when stored in the freezer.)

Make the caramel:
In a medium stainless-steel saucepan over medium-high heat, combine the sugar and ¼ cup water. Boil until the sugar has completely melted and taken on a light caramel color, about 10 minutes.

Remove from the heat. Slowly stir the orange juice and cream into the saucepan. Be careful: the caramel will sputter. Add the olives and the salt. Let the caramel cool slightly, then carefully puree in a blender or food processor until smooth. Work in batches if necessary. Cool completely. Serve at room temperature or slightly warmed. (This can be stored in the refrigerator for 5 days.)

To serve, unmold the chilled mousse and slice into 8 pieces. Serve with a dollop of the reserved whipped cream and a drizzle of the caramel. Serve the remaining caramel on the side.

2½ teaspoons unflavored powdered gelatin

6 tablespoons plus ⅓ cup sugar

2 cups mango puree

6 tablespoons fresh lemon juice

1 cup half-and-half

1 cup coconut cream

¼ teaspoon kosher salt

1 mango, peeled and medium diced

8 to 10 strawberries, hulled and sliced

A little while ago I was asked to cook for an event for pregnant women at a Chicago baby clothing boutique called Monica & Andy. The idea was to feature foods that were good for mama and baby during pregnancy, so I needed to do a little research for a "healthy" dessert. (I couldn't just serve enormous bowls of ice cream, which was my pregnancy go-to.) Mangoes are filled with all kinds of nutrients, and I also knew that the shopowner's mom is from India, where the fruit pops up in desserts all the time. So, I decided to riff on a dish our Duck Duck Goat pastry chef Nate created, topping sweet-and-tart mango jelly with a rich coconut cream that is as light and delicate as a cloud. *Serves 8*

MANGO PARFAIT
WITH COCONUT CLOUD

In a small bowl, combine half the gelatin with 2 tablespoons cold water. Set aside for 5 minutes.

In a small saucepan over low heat, combine 5 tablespoons of the sugar with 3 tablespoons water and cook until the sugar has completely dissolved, about 6 minutes. Add the mango puree and lemon juice, and heat until just warm. Remove the pan from the heat. Whisk in the reserved gelatin mixture until the gelatin has completely dissolved. Strain the liquid through a fine-mesh sieve into a medium bowl. Evenly distribute the mango mixture among 8 individual serving bowls. Refrigerate to set, at least 2 hours or up to 4 days.

In a small bowl, combine the remaining gelatin with ¼ cup of the half-and-half and set aside for 5 minutes.

In small saucepan over low heat, stir together ⅓ cup of the sugar, the remaining 1¾ cups half-and-half, the coconut cream, and salt, and cook until the sugar has completely dissolved and the mixture is warmed through, about 8 minutes. Whisk in the reserved gelatin mixture and strain through a fine-mesh sieve into a medium bowl. Refrigerate until slightly firm, at least 1 hour and up to 4 days.

(Continues)

Toss the diced mango and strawberries with the remaining 1 tablespoon sugar and allow them to macerate for about 15 minutes.

To serve, spoon the coconut cloud into an iSi canister and load with two chargers so you're guaranteed nice, fluffy results. Holding the canister at a 90-degree angle 1 inch above each serving of mango jelly, dispense the coconut cloud so it piles up into a nice pillow. (Alternatively, you can whip the coconut cloud in the bowl of a stand mixer for 10 minutes, then spoon a generous dollop of it onto the mango jelly.)

Garnish each serving with some of the macerated mango and strawberry slices.

CRUST

1½ cups finely broken
  chocolate sandwich
  cookies, filling removed
  (a.k.a. eaten)

2 tablespoons unsalted
  butter, melted, plus more
  if needed

1½ teaspoons sugar

⅛ teaspoon kosher salt

CURD

1 cup frozen passionfruit
  puree

3 large egg yolks

1 large egg

½ cup sugar

¼ vanilla bean, split
  lengthwise and seeds
  scraped

½ teaspoon fresh lemon
  juice

1 teaspoon unflavored
  powdered gelatin

1½ teaspoons warm water

4 tablespoons (½ stick)
  unsalted butter, cut into
  1-inch cubes

MERINGUE

2 large egg whites

2 tablespoons sugar

1½ tablespoons crushed
  cocoa nibs (optional)

I always loved lemon meringue pie. This is my version of the classic puckery dessert, with the addition of a chocolate-sandwich-cookie-crumb crust and passionfruit puree to balance the sweet meringue with fruity tartness. *Makes 1 (9-inch) pie*

PASSIONFRUIT MERINGUE PIE

Make the crust:
Preheat the oven to 375°F. In a large bowl, combine the cookie crumbs, butter, sugar, and salt and mix until the texture is homogenous and the crumbs form a ball when squeezed together. Add a little more melted butter to the mixture if it's too crumbly. Press the crust into a 9-inch pie pan and bake for 10 minutes, or until just set. Cool completely before filling.

Make the curd:
In a double boiler or a medium heatproof bowl set on top of a small pot of barely simmering water, combine the passionfruit puree, egg yolks, eggs, sugar, vanilla seeds, and lemon juice. Cook, whisking constantly, until very thick, 6 to 8 minutes. Make sure not to let the mixture overheat; otherwise, the eggs will scramble.

Strain the filling through a fine-mesh sieve into a large glass bowl. Stir the gelatin and warm water together in a small bowl and then whisk it into the curd. Add the butter one or two cubes at a time, while beating with a hand mixer or whisk. Cover the bowl with plastic wrap, pressing the plastic to the surface. Cool completely in the fridge, at least 3 hours or overnight.

Pour the chilled curd into the cooled crust (there will be a little leftover curd) and cover with plastic wrap. Refrigerate to allow the curd to set, at least 1 hour or overnight.

Make the meringue:
In a double boiler or a medium stainless-steel bowl set on top of a small pot of barely simmering water, whisk together the egg whites and sugar. Heat and whisk until the sugar has dissolved, 6 minutes. Pour the mixture into the bowl of a stand mixer fitted with the whisk attachment. Whip on high speed until stiff peaks form and the meringue is glossy. Fold in the cocoa nibs, if using.

Spread the meringue over the chilled curd and use a spatula or spoon to create peaks over the top. If desired, caramelize the top of the meringue with a kitchen torch until golden brown. Serve immediately.

I love making these mini pies because the dough can be shaped and filled with any fruit that's in season and has been tossed in a little sugar. These are really fun served with Cajeta Ice Cream (page 249). *Serves 4 to 6*

BLUEBERRY-STRAWBERRY HAND PIES

Make the crust:

Pulse the flour, salt, and granulated sugar in a food processor to combine. Add the butter a little at a time, and pulse until sandy in texture. There should still be small chunks of fat visible. Drizzle in the ice water and pulse until dough begins to come together. Remove from mixer and finish working the dough into a ball with your hands. Form the dough into a disc, wrap in plastic, and chill for at least an hour or up to 2 days.

Line 2 sheet pans with parchment paper. On a lightly floured surface, roll out the dough until ⅛ inch thick. Cut out eight 4-inch circles from the dough and transfer them to the prepared sheet pans. Chill until ready to use.

Make the filling:

In a large bowl, toss together the blueberries, strawberries, blackberries, granulated sugar, cornstarch, salt, and lemon juice and let sit for a few minutes.

Fill the center of each dough circle with a heaping pile of fruit, leaving an inch of clean edge around the fruit. Fold up a small section of the edge and pinch, as if you were pleating the crust. Repeat this process until the dough is pleated all the way around and holds its shape around the berries. The berries will be exposed on the top. Brush the outside of each pie with the egg wash and sprinkle with the turbinado sugar. Put the tarts in the freezer for 20 minutes. You can also store the unbaked pies in the fridge for a few hours.

Preheat the oven to 400°F.

Bake the tarts until the crust is golden brown and the fruit is bubbling, about 20 minutes. Serve warm.

CRUST

2 cups all-purpose flour

½ tablespoon salt

¼ cup granulated sugar

1 cup (2 sticks) unsalted butter, cut into small pieces and chilled

2 tablespoons ice cold water

FILLING

2 cups fresh blueberries

2 cups fresh strawberries, hulled and quartered

2 cups blackberries, halved lengthwise

1 cup granulated sugar

½ cup cornstarch

Pinch of salt

Juice of 1 lemon

1 egg white, beaten with a splash of water

¼ cup turbinado sugar, such as Sugar In The Raw

ICE CREAM for DINNER

. . . .

Even if you're not like me and don't treat yourself to a nightly bowl of ice cream, I bet you can imagine how much fun it would be if you skipped the savory stuff altogether and indulged some friends in a blowout ice cream sundae and cookie extravaganza. Put out a couple different ice creams that use the same simple base, plus a big spread of my take on classic toppings so your friends can mix and match. (Extra bonus: You get to keep all the leftovers.) You can add a cheeseboard and crackers, or party nuts to round things out, if you insist. Otherwise, I say go all-in on making your inner ten-year-old's dreams come true.

ICE CREAMS

Basic Recipe

One simple base recipe is all you need to make endless homemade ice cream creations. After churning, you can infuse the aerated cream base, swirl in jams or toffee or chocolate sauces, or add tasty bits like chocolate chunks or broken-up cake pieces. Just have fun with it! There is no need for a fancy and expensive ice cream maker here—any cheap model will work just fine. *Makes 1 quart*

2 cups heavy cream

1 cup whole milk

⅔ cup sugar

⅛ teaspoon kosher salt

4 large egg yolks

In a large saucepan over medium heat, combine the cream, milk, sugar, and salt, and bring to a simmer. Cook until the sugar dissolves, about 5 minutes. Turn off the heat.

In a medium bowl, break up the yolks with a whisk. Whisking constantly, slowly add about a third of the hot cream to the yolks, then whisk the yolk mixture back into the pan with the cream. Turn the heat to medium low and gently cook, stirring with a wooden spoon, until the mixture thickens and coats the back of the spoon, 6 to 8 minutes. Strain through a fine-mesh sieve into a bowl set over a bowl of ice cubes and let cool to room temperature.

Cover with plastic and chill for at least 4 hours or overnight. Follow the manufacturer's instructions for churning the ice cream. Transfer to a container and freeze for at least 1 hour or up to 2 weeks before serving.

Mint Chocolate Chip

Mint ice cream is great, but mint ice cream made with fresh mint instead of mint extract? Pretty much the best thing ever. There's also such a thing as chocolate mint, which actually tastes like the herb has chocolate in it. If you can find it, I highly recommend using it in this recipe. Otherwise, any fresh mint will do, or even basil. Then throw in some shaved chocolate for good measure, which doesn't get as crunchy as chocolate chips when frozen.

Follow the Basic Recipe, adding ½ cup tightly packed mint leaves to the cream and milk while they heat. After the ice cream has been churned, stir in ¾ cup shaved chocolate (just take a box grater to your favorite chocolate bar) before freezing.

Blueberry Swirl

Follow the Basic Recipe. While the ice cream is churning and almost set, spoon in ½ cup blueberry jam (see page 134, or use store-bought).

Salted Peanut

Like decadent, frozen peanut butter.

When making the base for the Basic Recipe, simmer the heavy cream and milk with 1 cup salted roasted peanuts.

Fennel-Orange

Fennel makes a surprising addition to a dessert, but if you think about its light, aniselike flavor, it's really no different from a little pop of black licorice. Add some citrus to brighten things up, and you have a refreshing, creamy treat.

When making the base for the Basic Recipe, simmer the cream and milk with ½ cup thinly sliced fresh fennel bulb and 1 tablespoon toasted fennel seeds. Just before churning, add the grated zest of 1 orange.

Cajeta

Cajeta is caramel made with goat's milk. You can buy it (you'd need 1 cup here), but I say if you're going to make your own ice cream, you might as well go the extra mile and make cajeta. Drizzle the cajeta into the base right before it's done churning. The end result is rich, a little nutty, and the tiniest bit spicy from a little black pepper.

2 cups goat's milk

⅓ cup sugar

¼ teaspoon baking soda

In a medium saucepan over medium-low heat, combine the ingredients and cook at a light simmer, whisking occasionally, until the mixture turns a light caramel color and the liquid is reduced by almost half, about 30 minutes. Allow to cool fully.

Follow the Basic Recipe, adding ¼ teaspoon freshly ground black pepper to the base, once it's cooled. While the ice cream is churning and almost set, drizzle in the cajeta.

TOPPINGS

Mom's Chocolate Fudge Sauce

When I asked my dad to send me my mom's old recipe, he couldn't remember her making a fudge sauce until I said, "You know, the stuff she made in the yellow pot, then put in the fridge for all of us to eat with a spoon for days afterward?" That magical pot of fudgy, chocolatey goodness was a million times better than store-bought sauce, and making it means having a few days' worth of midday finger scoops and midnight munchies.

Makes 3 cups

2 cups confectioners' sugar

4 ounces unsweetened chocolate, melted

⅔ cup evaporated milk

3 tablespoons unsalted butter

¼ teaspoon kosher salt

½ teaspoon vanilla extract

In a small saucepan over low heat, combine the confectioners' sugar and the melted chocolate. Gradually stir in the milk, continuing to stir until the sugar is completely dissolved and the sauce is smooth, about 8 minutes. Add the butter and salt, and cook, stirring continuously, until the sauce emulsifies, 10 minutes. Stir in the vanilla. Let the sauce cool completely, then cover and refrigerate until needed, or for up to 1 week. To serve, gently reheat and serve warm.

Chocolate Crunch

This reminds me of the ice cream cakes you get from Carvel (if you're from the East Coast, you totally know what I'm talking about). They always had a crunch layer that was like a mashup of chocolate chips and sprinkles. I learned pretty quickly to request the teddy bear birthday cake because the whole tummy of the bear was made of these tasty crunchy bits.

Makes 3 cups

1 cup (2 sticks) unsalted butter, cold and cubed

2 cups all-purpose flour

¼ cup sugar

2 tablespoons unsweetened cocoa powder

1½ teaspoons kosher salt

Preheat the oven to 350°F. Line a jelly roll pan (any size is fine) with parchment paper.

In the bowl of a stand mixer fitted with the paddle attachment or in a large bowl with a hand mixer or a spoon, mix the butter, flour, sugar, cocoa powder, and salt on low speed or slow spooning until all the butter is incorporated but the mixture is still crumbly.

Pour the butter mixture into the prepared pan and bake until slightly dried, 10 to 15 minutes. Cool completely and then crumble into bite-size pieces. Store in an airtight container for up to 1 week.

Inside-Out Malt Balls

Think of the perfect malt milkshake, or Whoppers that have been turned inside out so the chocolate is on the inside and the malty goodness is on the outside. So easy. So tasty.

Makes 4 cups

12 ounces quality milk chocolate

½ cup heavy cream

½ tablespoon light corn syrup

¼ teaspoon kosher salt

1 tablespoon unsalted butter, at room temperature

⅓ cup malted milk powder

Line a large baking sheet with a silicone baking mat.

In a double boiler or a medium glass or metal bowl set on top of a small pot of simmering water, warm the chocolate, cream, corn syrup, and salt. Whisk constantly until the ingredients are melted and emulsified. Add the butter and whisk until completely smooth. Spread the chocolate mixture onto the prepared pan and freeze for at least 1 hour and up to 2 weeks.

In a cool room (ideally), carefully portion out the mixture into 1-inch balls with a melon baller or measuring spoon. Use your hands to roll until smooth. Toss the balls in the malted milk powder. Put on the lined tray in a single layer and store, covered, in the fridge or freezer for up to 5 days.

Brown Sugar–Cayenne Caramel

Just a tiny bit of cayenne pepper helps give this sweet caramel a surprising little kick.

Makes 2 cups

8 tablespoons (1 stick) unsalted butter

1 cup dark brown sugar

¾ cup heavy cream

½ teaspoon kosher salt

⅛ teaspoon cayenne pepper

In a small saucepan over medium heat, melt the butter. Add the brown sugar and simmer for

5 minutes without stirring. Pour in the cream and whisk to incorporate. Cook for 10 minutes, until the sugar completely dissolves. Add the salt and pepper and whisk to combine. Serve while warm or let the caramel cool completely before storing in an airtight container in the fridge for up to 5 days.

Spread the popcorn on the prepared baking sheet and top with the second sheet of parchment, sprayed side down. Press the popcorn into a thin layer either using your hands or with another baking sheet. Let the caramel cool completely.

Break into bite-size pieces. Store in an airtight container at room temperature for up to 1 week.

Caramel Popcorn Crunch

I was always more of a cheesy popcorn lover than a caramel corn fan—until one of my pastry chefs started making fresh caramel corn. Instead of that greasy, semi-toffee-flavored tinned stuff, this is the real deal: sweet, salty, and crunchy.

Makes about 4 cups

Nonstick cooking spray
8 cups popped popcorn
4 cups sugar
½ tablespoon kosher salt
2 tablespoons unsalted butter

Line a large baking sheet with parchment paper and cover in nonstick cooking spray. Spray a second sheet of parchment.

In a food processor, pulse the popcorn until broken into small pieces.

In a large nonreactive saucepan over medium-high heat, cook the sugar until completely melted, 6 to 8 minutes. Continue cooking without stirring until the sugar is a deep caramel color, about 10 more minutes. Remove the pan from the heat and carefully add the salt and butter to the caramel (it'll steam and bubble up). Whisk until the caramel thickens, lightens in color, and emulsifies. Switch to a wooden spoon, add the popcorn, and stir until it's completely coated.

Toasted Marshmallow Creme

This is for the Fluff lover in all of us.

Makes 2 cups

Nonstick cooking spray
1 (16-ounce) bag mini marshmallows
½ cup heavy cream
½ teaspoon vanilla extract
Generous pinch of salt

Lightly spray a 16 by 11-inch jelly roll pan with nonstick cooking spray. Spread the marshmallows in a single layer on the prepared pan. Using a torch or running the pan under a preheated broiler, toast the marshmallows until they are uniformly golden brown and starting to melt. A couple of small burnt spots are fine.

Scrape the toasted marshmallows into a small saucepan over medium heat. Add the cream, vanilla, and salt, and bring to a boil while whisking constantly. Remove from the heat and let the sauce cool slightly. If not serving immediately, cool the sauce completely before storing it in an airtight container in the fridge, and reheat when ready to use.

COOKIES

Chocolate Chunk

A total classic. *Makes 36 cookies*

3¼ cups all-purpose flour

2 teaspoons kosher salt

¾ teaspoon baking soda

1 cup (2 sticks) unsalted butter, at room temperature

1 cup plus 2½ tablespoons light brown sugar

⅔ cup granulated sugar

2 large eggs

4 teaspoons vanilla extract

1 cup dark chocolate chunks

1 cup milk chocolate chunks

In a medium bowl, whisk together the flour, salt, and baking soda.

In the bowl of a stand mixer fitted with the paddle attachment, beat the butter, brown sugar, and granulated sugar on medium-high speed until well combined and fluffy. Add the eggs one at a time, mixing completely after each addition. Stream in the vanilla, then scrape down the sides of the bowl. On low speed, add the flour mixture and mix until almost fully combined. Switch to a wooden spoon or a spatula to gently fold in the dark and milk chocolate chunks. Cover the bowl with plastic wrap and refrigerate the dough for 30 minutes.

Preheat the oven to 325°F. Line a sheet tray with parchment paper.

Portion the dough out in 3-tablespoon scoops spaced 2 inches apart on the prepared tray. Bake until completely set but still soft in the center, 12 to 15 minutes. Allow the cookies to cool completely on the sheet tray before moving them to a wire rack. (Store in a zip tight bag for up to 3 days.)

Oatmeal-Cranberry

I like my oatmeal cookies to be on the chewier side than the usual crisp, crumbly versions. I also like adding tart cranberries versus raisins, which end up being too sweet for an already sweet cookie. *Makes 24 cookies*

2 cups rolled oats, old-fashioned or quick

2 cups all-purpose flour

1¾ cups granulated sugar

1 cup light brown sugar

½ teaspoon baking soda

½ teaspoon baking powder

1 teaspoon kosher salt

1 cup (2 sticks) unsalted butter, at room temperature

2 large eggs

1 teaspoon vanilla extract

¾ cup dried cranberries

In a large bowl, whisk together the oats, flour, sugars, baking soda, baking powder, and salt.

In the bowl of a stand mixer fitted with the paddle attachment, beat the butter on medium speed until light, about 3 minutes. Add the eggs and vanilla, and mix for 1 minute. On low speed, slowly add the oat mixture and mix until just combined, about 1 minute. Switch to a wooden spoon and fold in the cranberries. Cover the bowl with plastic wrap and refrigerate the dough for 1 hour.

Preheat the oven to 325°F. Line two cookie sheets with parchment paper.

Using your hands, portion the dough out into 2-tablespoon balls. Arrange the cookies on the baking sheets 2 inches apart. Bake until golden brown, 12 to 14 minutes. Allow the cookies to cool completely before moving them to a wire rack. (Store in a zippered bag for up to 3 days.)

Peanut Butter Sandwich

I've always been a a sucker for a good peanut butter cookie, which is why I was so excited that my former pastry chef Matthew created these, which are inspired by the ones you'd make as a kid and mark on top with a fork. They have that same intense peanut butter flavor but an even better duo of textures—chewy and crispy—plus a creamy frosting filling.

Makes 12 sandwich cookies

COOKIES

2⅓ cups all-purpose flour

1 cup old-fashioned oats

2 teaspoons kosher salt

1 teaspoon baking soda

1 cup (2 sticks) unsalted butter, at room temperature

1 cup light brown sugar

1 cup granulated sugar

2 large eggs

2 teaspoons vanilla extract

1¾ cups creamy peanut butter

FILLING

1 cup (2 sticks) unsalted butter, at room temperature

¾ cup creamy peanut butter

1 cup plus 1 tablespoon confectioners' sugar, sifted

Make the cookies:
In a large bowl, whisk together the flour, oats, salt, and baking soda.

In the bowl of a stand mixer fitted with the paddle attachment, beat the butter and both sugars on medium-high speed until well combined and fluffy. Add the eggs one at a time, mixing completely after each addition. Add the vanilla and peanut butter. Mix completely and scrape down the sides of the bowl. On low speed, add the flour mixture and mix until just combined. Cover the bowl and refrigerate the dough for 20 minutes.

Divide the dough in half. Put each half between 2 sheets of parchment paper and roll out until ⅛ inch thick. Portion the dough into 2-tablespoon scoops and flatten until ⅛ inch thick with the smooth bottom of a drinking glass. Lay the cookies on parchment-lined baking sheets, placing them 1 inch apart, and freeze for 2 hours.

Preheat the oven to 325°F.

Bake the cookies until golden brown, 10 minutes. Cool completely on the baking sheets before moving to a wire rack and filling.

Make the filling:
In the bowl of a stand mixer fitted with the whisk attachment, whip the butter and peanut butter until soft and smooth. On low speed, add the confectioners' sugar and mix until combined. Scrape down the sides of the bowl and whip on high speed until light and fluffy, 2 to 3 minutes. Transfer the filling to a piping bag with a ¼-inch tip.

Lay half of the cookies flat side up on a smooth surface. Pipe the filling onto the center of each cookie, leaving a ¼-inch border. Top with a naked cookie, flat side down, and press down to squish the filling to the edge. Serve at room temperature. (Store on a plate or sheet tray, wrapped tightly in plastic, for up to 3 days.)

Wookie Pies

These are my take on chocolate cookie whoopie pies. I first made them a long time ago (in a galaxy in the West Loop) for a May 4th *Star Wars*–themed party at Little Goat. (May the fourth be with you!) They don't do a ton of tasty eating in the movies that I could use as inspiration, but my cooks and I managed to come up with fun dishes like Masa the Hut, Obi Naan, and Ewok Empanadas. Oh, and we served a green Yoda cocktail (which, you'll notice, is a recipe that did not make it into this book). Anyway, whether or not you're a total *Star Wars* nerd like me, these are still a chocolate lover's dream: fluffy chocolate cake filled with creamy chocolate icing.

Makes 12 sandwich cookies

COOKIES

4 cups all-purpose flour

1½ cups unsweetened cocoa powder

2 teaspoons baking soda

1 teaspoon kosher salt

8 tablespoons (1 stick) unsalted butter, at room temperature

2 cups light brown sugar

2 large eggs, at room temperature

1 cup buttermilk

FILLING

8 tablespoons (1 stick) unsalted butter, at room temperature

1¾ cups confectioners' sugar

2½ tablespoons unsweetened cocoa powder

2½ tablespoons malted milk powder

1½ tablespoons buttermilk powder or milk powder

¼ teaspoon kosher salt

2½ tablespoons whole milk

1 teaspoon vanilla extract

Preheat the oven to 300°F. Line a baking sheet with parchment paper.

Make the cookies:
In a large bowl, whisk together the flour, cocoa powder, baking soda, and salt.

In the bowl of a stand mixer fitted with the paddle attachment, beat the butter and sugar on medium-high speed until well combined and fluffy. Add the eggs, mixing well between additions. Scrape down the sides of the bowl. Reduce the speed to low and add one-third of the flour mixture, then ½ cup of the buttermilk. Scrape the bowl again and add half of the remaining flour mixture and the rest of the buttermilk before mixing in the last of the flour. Mix just until combined (it will be very thick). Detach the bowl from the mixer and scrape the bottom to make sure the batter is uniform.

Portion the batter in 3-tablespoon scoops and put 2 inches apart on the prepared sheet tray. Bake until completely set but still soft, 10 to 12 minutes. Let cool completely on the sheet tray before transferring to a wire rack.

Make the filling:
In the bowl of a stand mixer fitted with the whisk attachment, whip the butter on medium-high speed until soft and smooth, 2 minutes. Sift in the confectioners' sugar, cocoa powder, malted milk powder, buttermilk powder, and salt, and mix on low speed until combined. Drizzle in the milk and vanilla, and mix until completely combined. Scrape down the sides and bottom of the bowl before whipping the ingredients on high speed until light and fluffy, 3 minutes. Transfer the filling to a piping bag with a ½-inch tip.

Lay half the cookies flat side up on a smooth surface. Pipe the filling onto the center of each cookie, leaving a ½-inch border. Top with a naked cookie, flat side down, and press down to squish the filling to the edge. Serve at room temperature. (Store wookies on a plate or baking sheet, wrapped in plastic, for up to 3 days.)

PICKLED THINGS

PICKLES SHOW UP IN THE VAST MAJORITY OF MY DISHES BECAUSE they add the perfect briny, tangy, bright note that just kinda brings all the other flavors together. I believe the perfect pickle doesn't overpower a dish when you bite into it; rather it accentuates everything else that is hanging out with it. I've been known to pickle just about anything—from peppers to watermelon rinds—so this chapter highlights only a few of my (incredibly simple) favorites.

PICKLED RED ONIONS

I don't love adding raw onions to a dish—they can be a little intense—but when you pickle them, their natural sweetness comes out. Use the pickled onions themselves anywhere you would put regular sliced onions, such as on sandwiches, tacos, or salads, or use the pickling liquid and a little olive oil to make a vinaigrette. *Makes 1½ cups*

2 cups thinly sliced red onions

1 teaspoon coriander seeds

1 teaspoon black peppercorns

2 cups red wine vinegar

1 cup sugar

2 tablespoons salt

Put the onions in a heatproof storage container with a lid.

In the bottom of a medium saucepan over medium heat, toast the coriander and black peppercorns until fragrant, 4 to 5 minutes. Add the vinegar, sugar, salt, and ½ cup water. Bring to a boil and then remove the pot from the heat. Strain the liquid over the onions.

Ensuring that the onions are completely submerged, weight them down with a small plate or bowl, and let cool to room temperature. The pickles can be stored in the refrigerator, in their liquid, for up to 2 weeks.

PICKLED CARROTS

So simple and so tasty. Carrots are naturally full of sugar, so the acidity of the pickling liquid gives them a great tangy, balanced flavor. I love adding pickled carrots to slaws, tuna or chicken salad, pasta, or just straight up on my sandwich or burger. *Makes 2 cups*

¾ cup seasoned rice wine vinegar

3 cups shredded carrots

In a large saucepan over medium-high heat, bring the vinegar to a boil and remove from the heat.

Put the carrots in a heatproof container and pour the vinegar over them. Let cool to room temperature. Cover and refrigerate for up to 1 month.

KIMCHI

This is an inauthentic version of the Korean condiment (it's vegan, for starters), but it's got that same funky, pickle goodness that makes this a favorite pairing with grilled meats, simple fish dishes, and of course, eggs (see page 14). *Makes 4 cups*

1 head napa cabbage, cut into 1-inch pieces

1 small head bok choy, cut into 1-inch pieces

½ cup salt

2 garlic cloves

1 (½-inch) piece fresh ginger, peeled

6 scallions, cut into 1-inch pieces (white and green parts)

6 garlic chives, cut into 1-inch pieces

1 cup Kimchi Sauce (recipe follows), or more to taste

1 teaspoon crushed red pepper flakes, preferably Korean, or to taste

3 tablespoons toasted sesame seeds

Put the cabbage and bok choy pieces in a large bowl or zippered bag. Evenly distribute the salt over the vegetables and toss well. Refrigerate overnight.

The next day, drain off the liquid, reserving ½ cup. Combine the garlic, ginger, and reserved liquid in a blender and blend to a smooth paste.

In a large bowl, toss together the scallions, chives, sauce, red pepper flakes, sesame seeds, the garlic-ginger paste, and the cabbage mixture. If you prefer your kimchi spicier and fuller flavored, add ¼ cup more sauce. Cover and allow the kimchi to sit overnight in a cool, dry place at room temperature. It'll be ready to use in the morning! The kimchi can be stored in the refrigerator for up to 2 weeks.

Kimchi Sauce

Makes 2 cups

2 tablespoons soy sauce

1 tablespoon minced garlic

1 tablespoon minced fresh ginger

3 tablespoons gochujang chile paste

3 tablespoons doenjang soybean paste (a fermented soybean product) or brown miso paste

¼ cup malt vinegar

1½ tablespoons dark brown sugar

⅛ teaspoon crushed red pepper flakes, preferably Korean, or to taste

Combine the soy sauce, garlic, and ginger in a blender and blend until smooth. Add the remaining ingredients and blend until fully combined. Store in an airtight container in the refrigerator for up to 1 week.

PICKLED HUNGARIAN HOTS AND BANANAS

Since I'm not a huge fan of crazy, fiery spice, I like to take Hungarian hot peppers—which are super spicy—and mix them with sweeter banana peppers to end up with a mix that adds a little kick but isn't too in your face. I love how you can actually taste the natural sweetness and fresh "greenness" of the peppers. Try them heaped onto a grilled steak or in fajitas, as a topping over fried rice, or chopped up into a pickle relish. *Makes 2 cups*

2 cups champagne vinegar

¾ cup sugar

¼ cup salt

3 banana peppers, seeded and sliced into thin rings

3 Hungarian peppers, seeded and sliced into thin rings

In a medium saucepan over medium-high heat, bring the vinegar, sugar, and salt to a boil.

Put the peppers in a heatproof container with a fitted lid. Pour the hot pickling liquid over the peppers and let cool to room temperature, making sure the peppers are fully submerged in the liquid.

When completely cool, cover the peppers and refrigerate for up to 1 month.

PICKLED WATERMELON RIND

My sous chefs helped me find the perfect recipe by taking all their grandmas' recipes and combining them into a not-too-sweet pickle with a crunchy texture. We like to use them to lighten up heavier meat dishes. *Makes 4 cups*

Rind of 1 medium watermelon (pink flesh removed)

1 cup salt

1 tablespoon food-grade calcium chloride (a common canning ingredient found in many grocery stores or online)

6 cups sugar

4 cups apple cider vinegar

1 cinnamon stick

2 dried Thai chiles

1 tablespoon coriander seeds

1 star anise

Using a sharp knife or vegetable peeler, peel the green skin from the rind. Cut the rind into ¼-inch-thick pieces (the size and shape of the pieces will vary).

In a large bowl or container, combine the salt and calcium chloride with 2 quarts warm water and stir until dissolved. Add the rind, cool for a few minutes, cover, and refrigerate for 72 hours.

Drain the liquid from the rind. In a large pot over low heat, combine the rind with the sugar, vinegar, cinnamon, chiles, coriander, anise, and 3 quarts water. Simmer until the rinds are translucent and soft, 1½ hours. Cool completely, then cover and refrigerate for up to 1 month.

PICKLED FRESNO CHILES

A little spicy, a little fresh, and really, really bright, these are great sliced thin and tossed into salads or sauces, or on avocado toast.

Makes 1 cup

⅔ cup champagne vinegar

¼ cup sugar

1 teaspoon salt

1 cup sliced and seeded fresh Fresno chiles

In a medium saucepan over medium-high heat, bring the vinegar, sugar, and salt to a boil. Put the chiles in a heatproof container, pour the pickling liquid on top, and allow to cool to room temperature. Cover and store in the fridge for up to 1 month.

BREAD AND BUTTER PICKLES

Growing up in Connecticut, I knew that when you got pickles on your sandwiches, it was always the sweet bread-and-butter ones, not the briny dills; I really like that layer of sweet crunch piled on with other toppings. These are also a staple on my cheeseboards because of how nicely they play with salty, creamy cheeses and crackers. Or you could dip them in tempura batter and fry them, which is what I do at Little Goat. *Makes 6 cups*

¼ cup mustard seeds

½ tablespoon dill seeds

1 teaspoon whole cloves

2 quarts apple cider vinegar

4 cups light brown sugar

¾ cup salt

2 tablespoons ground turmeric

1 tablespoon ginger powder

½ tablespoon garlic powder

1 tablespoon food-grade calcium chloride

2 pounds pickling cucumbers, sliced in ¼-inch-thick rings

2 pounds sweet onions, sliced in 1-inch-thick rings

In a medium saucepan over medium heat, toast the mustard seeds, dill seeds, and cloves. Add the vinegar, brown sugar, salt, turmeric, ginger powder, garlic powder, calcium chloride, and 2 cups of water, and bring to boil. Stir to dissolve the sugar and salt.

Put the cucumbers and onions in a heatproof bowl. Using a fine-mesh strainer, strain the pickling liquid over them. Cool to room temperature. Cover and refrigerate for up to 1 month.

PICKLED JALAPEÑOS

Pickling tones down the heat level of these guys, giving them more brightness than overwhelming spice. That said, I do also add a bit of harissa to the pickling liquid, which adds a different layer of peppery flavor. These are great on top of a burger, especially cheeseburgers (and especially if you're like me and put mayo on your burger), because they cut through the richness. *Makes 3 cups*

2 cups distilled white vinegar

¾ cup sugar

¼ cup salt

1 teaspoon harissa, homemade (page 58) or store-bought

1 pound jalapeño chiles, sliced into ¼-inch rings

In a small saucepan over medium-high heat, bring the vinegar to a boil. Whisk in the sugar and salt and let dissolve. Remove from the heat and whisk in the harissa.

Put the chiles in a heatproof container, pour the pickling liquid over them, and let cool to room temperature. Cover and refrigerate for up to 1 month.

PICKLED SHALLOTS

Shallots have always played a huge part in my kitchens, though usually in a supporting role in sauces and vinaigrettes. Then I realized that when I pickle them, all that intense onion flavor melds with their natural sweetness. So, now they've been promoted to more of a starring role, making appearances in salads and sandwiches that need a nice, bright pick-me-up. Plus, they turn a really pretty pink color, so it's like adding a sprinkling of confetti to a dish. *Makes 1 cup*

½ cup champagne vinegar

3 tablespoons sugar

1½ teaspoons salt

2 cups thinly sliced shallots

In a small saucepan over medium-high heat, bring the vinegar and ¼ cup water to a boil. Add the sugar and salt, and whisk to dissolve.

Put the shallots in a heatproof container, pour the pickling liquid over them, and let cool to room temperature. Cover and refrigerate for up to 1 month.

PICKLED RHUBARB

Every year I eagerly await spring so we can
load up the kitchen with pickled rhubarb—
hopefully enough to last us until the following
spring. Rhubarb is naturally tart, so there's
a little bit of sweetness in the pickling liquid
to keep things balanced. It's important not
to pour the liquid over the rhubarb while it's
still hot or it won't stay crunchy. Use pickled
rhubarb in salsas, tapenades, and salads, or
anywhere you want a nice sweet, tart addition.
Makes 4 cups

1½ cups apple cider vinegar

¾ cup sugar

4 cups sliced rhubarb

1 sprig of tarragon

In a medium saucepan over medium-high heat,
bring the vinegar and sugar to a boil. Allow the
pickling liquid to cool to room temperature.
Put the rhubarb and tarragon in a container
with a fitted lid and pour the pickling liquid
over the top. Cover and store in the fridge for
up to 1 month.

ACKNOWLEDGMENTS

BIGGEST THANKS TO:

Nicki for testing recipes and handling more than I even know. You will always have more patience than I do!

Huge for shooting one of his first books with us. I think we both learned and grew from the process.

Rachel for taking my words and making them sound better.

Katie for keeping life organized, and for running out every time we needed a better-looking piece of fruit or a beer.

Shannon for just always being awesome!

Johanna for having such a beautiful collection of serving dishes and cook-ware and a great eye.

Gary, Ernie, and Burt for being my family. I love you!

INDEX

All rights reserved.
Published in the United States by **Clarkson Potter/
Publishers,** an imprint of the **Crown Publishing Group,**
a division of **Penguin Random House LLC,** New York.
clarksonpotter.com

CLARKSON POTTER is a trademark and **POTTER** with
colophon is a registered trademark of **Penguin Random
House LLC.**

Library of Congress Cataloging-in-Publication Data
Names: Izard, Stephanie, author. | Holtzman, Rachel,
    author.
Title: Gather and graze
    Stephanie Izard with Rachel Holtzman.
Description: First edition. | New York : Clarkson Potter/
    Publishers [2018] | Includes index.
Identifiers: LCCN 2017015346| ISBN 9780451495945 |
    ISBN 9780451495952 (eISBN)
Subjects: LCSH: Barbecuing. | Outdoor cooking. | LCGFT:
    Cookbooks.
Classification: LCC TX840.B3 I85 2018 | DDC 641.5/784—
    dc23
LC record available at https://lccn.loc.gov/2017015346

ISBN 978-0-451-49594-5
Ebook ISBN 978-0-451-49595-2

Printed in China

Book and cover design by **Ian Dingman**

10 9 8 7 6 5 4 3 2 1

First Edition